W9-BJS-149

JUST SAY
THE WORD!

A Fascinating Collection of
Popular Expressions
From the Bible

Steven Melvin McCalip

Dedicated to all those who believe
"The law of the LORD *is* perfect, converting
the soul: the testimony of LORD *is* sure,
making wise the simple...More to be desired
are they than gold, yea, than much fine gold:
Sweeter also than honey, and the
honeycomb." (Psalm 19:7,10)

Published by
God's Treasure Chest
Alief, Texas

Printed in the USA by Far East Printing
Cover graphics by Refugio Martinez
Cover design by Steven McCalip

Order form and information on pages 255-256
To order additional copies for yourself
or a business, please visit the website, e-mail, fax, or write:

www.godstreasurechest.com or godstreasure@ev1.net

or fax (713) 718-6180

or write
God's Treasure Chest
P.O. Box 2053
Alief, Texas 77411-2053

ISBN 0-9711505-0-8

Contents

Preface

It's been stated that there have been more books written about the Bible than any other topic. Of all those books, I have seen only a handful that touched on the topic of popular expressions occurring in the Bible. However, none of those books covered the topic to the extent and in the manner I thought the Bible deserved. Some of these books bogged down the reader with archaic words and literary allusions from the Bible (i.e., "husbandman," "sottish," "burning bush," "lilies of the field," etc.) and some emphasized popular quotations like "O ye of little faith" and "why hast thou forsaken me?"

I wanted my book to focus solely on popular expressions, so I set out to find as many popular expressions that occurred in the Bible as I could. I also wanted to distinguish popular expressions in current usage and those more popular from other generations. It was an exhausting but thoroughly enjoyable task. Reading through just about every occurrence of every word in *Strong's Exhaustive Concordance of the Bible* can be tedious to say the least. Reading through the entire Bible again in my search for these phrases, however, was very rewarding. The excitement of discovering new phrases was half the fun. Even after several years and hundreds of expressions later, I am to this day still finding more in the Bible. I'm sure the reader will share the joy of finding new ones as well.

I think *JUST SAY THE WORD!* is another example of why the Bible itself is such a unique and influential book. It is my love for the King James Bible that gave me the desire to have this work published. I can't tell you how many times these expressions have opened the door to discuss the deeper issues of the Bible with others. I want to acknowledge the many friends and family members that encouraged me to stick to this project and see its completion. It truly was a "labor of love" given to me by the Lord for his book.

Introduction

Throughout recorded history, perhaps no language has exercised such worldwide influence as that of English. Over the last 500 years, English has become the universal tongue and official language in world politics, public education, scientific research, and international commerce. Even more importantly, it has become the primary or secondary language in a large number of countries today.

When one considers the impact of the English language, a question worth pondering is this: What propelled and contributed to English becoming such a dominant language in the world? The rise of England to world power through its global colonization is the first reason that might come to mind. What is not given its just due, however, is the influence of England's Bible, the King James Version, on our written and spoken English.

Translated in 1611, the King James Bible soon became the standard of all bibles. It has been, and continues to be, the single greatest selling and most widely distributed book of all time. It is, as some have aptly said, "the book that shook the world." Its contributions to Western literature are practically immeasurable, being mentioned by many of the world's most renowned writers as having a profound effect on them and their writings. The individual books of Job and Psalms, among others, have been called the finest examples of poetry ever penned, and this is said by many who don't hold to Christianity as their religion.

Although there is a great need to show all of the various contributions of the King James Bible on the English language, one aspect that deserves particular attention is the influence of this particular Bible on our common speech. Whether we be Christian, Muslim, Buddhist, agnostic, or atheist, we all incorporate a host of biblical sayings into our daily conversations.

The English language is replete with idioms, sayings, and expressions of which a surprising number originate or were made popular from the King James Bible. This book has become imbedded in our common speech, yet people speak biblical phrases daily without realizing they're quoting or alluding directly from the King James Bible. Sayings such as "rise and shine," "give up the ghost," "the skin of your teeth," "see eye to eye," "safe and sound," and "eat, drink, and be merry" are just several of the hundreds of examples in this work.

Quite to the contrary of some scholarly opinions, the King James Bible is far from archaic and is anything but outdated. In fact, in light of the number of current expressions used in it, this book could be said to be one of the most up-to-date you can read. The King James Bible is the most widely recognized, the most widely memorized, and the most widely read book in the world. The book speaks for itself quite literally. It is "high time" (Romans 13:11) that we recognize its hold on our language.

Jesus said, "...the words that I speak unto you, *they* are spirit, and *they* are life." Despite being thousands of years old, his words are most assuredly living in today's language. Well-known expressions such as "the blind leading the blind," "the powers that be," and "fall by the wayside," are, as the book of Isaiah itself says, "a drop in the bucket" compared to the 500 more popular sayings that are in our Bible.

It is my belief that a majority of these expressions did come or were made popular from scripture. I base this opinion mainly on the Bible's age and its pervasive influence on many languages, especially English. The manuscripts that produced the King James Bible go back as far as 3,500 years. Most of recorded history itself begins not long before that, so the Bible has been influencing the language of mankind for longer that just about any other written source.

In preparing this book, I chose the expressions that I felt were most often used based on my personal experience and research. The expressions used are all considered to be popular at one time or another by authorities in the field of linguistics. All scripture quotations are from the King James

Bible and include the old spelling, grammar, and italics found in it.

A major portion of this work was dedicated to showing the biblical context of these phrases. Each phrase is highlighted in the scripture in which it occurs, and each phrase's meaning (when not obvious) is discussed as well. The subject matter of the surrounding verses and their sometimes controversial doctrines are often discussed. It is not my intention to promote strife or antagonize, only to give my understanding of the context of these phrases and how they relate to the issues of the day. If the commentary "ruffles a few feathers," then so be it, "for if I yet pleased men, I should not be the servant of Christ."

Throughout this book, you will not only be surprised at the various expressions that are found in scripture, but you will also be amazed at the numerous examples of popular sentiment that are shown to be at odds with the Bible. The popularity of these expressions is contrasted with the unpopularity of the doctrinal context in which they occur.

The reader will appreciate the various appendixes he will find in this work that show more expressions and their cultural usage. Appendix A lists expressions that were more popular in early years, and Appendix B includes phrases that are alluded to in the Bible; i.e., those that are hinted at but that are not directly stated. Appendixes C and D show how these expressions have been used in movie and song titles in Western culture. Not included is a list of book titles having biblical expressions, for that could have filled another whole book. Suffice it to say that thousands of these expressions have been used as the titles of books over the years. If you are a writer trying to come up with a title for a book, article, or headline, look no further than a copy of the Bible.

It is my hope that after you have read this work, you will gain a greater appreciation for the grandeur of the King James Bible and its profound linguistic, cultural, and spiritual impact on American society and the world.

Steven Melvin McCalip

A

act of God

> But your eyes have seen all the great **acts of the Lord** which he did. (Deuteronomy 11:7)

Moses reminded Israel of all the "great acts of the Lord" which they had seen including the drowning of Pharaoh and his army in the Red Sea. Also called a great act of the Lord was the literal opening up of the earth and the swallowing of the households of Dathan and Abiram for their rebellion against God.

This incident foreshadowed the fate of the wicked who will actually be cast into the same place as Dathan and Abiram's household—the middle of the earth, or hell, according to many scriptures. Psalm 55:15 says the wicked "go down quick into hell," and Jesus said in Luke 10:15 that people are "thrust down to hell." "The way of life *is* above to the wise, that he may depart from hell beneath" (Proverbs 15:24).

Insurance companies today refuse to cover acts of God, or natural calamities, as they label it. Apparently, they aren't responsible for what God does. The Lord offers fire and life insurance of a different sort, but unlike others, he covers "acts of God."

all things are possible

> And Jesus looking upon them saith, With men *it is* impossible, but not with God: for with God **all things are possible**. (Mark 10:27)

People like to think that all things are possible concerning man's abilities, but according to the Bible, the phrase "all things are possible" is true only with God. Jesus made this statement in response to a question from his disciples as to whom could be saved. The Lord had just told them that it was very difficult for a rich man to enter heaven, but with God this was not impossible. If nothing were impossible for man, we wouldn't need God. We should be thankful for the things that are impossible for us, for these things force us to go to God.

all things to all men

> To the weak became I as weak, that I might gain the weak: I am made **all things to all _men_**, that I might by all means save some. (1 Corinthians 9:22)

This expression is mistakenly understood by some Christians to mean that beliefs can be compromised in order to get along with others for the ultimate purpose of getting people saved. A Christian doesn't lie in order to befriend a liar; he doesn't become worldly in order to win the world. Paul spoke of winning souls, not by any means necessary, but by becoming a servant to others. The seasoned saint learns to become all things to all men by taking on the different roles of a Christian such as a teacher who explains the scriptures, a fisherman who fishes for souls, a farmer who tends his crops, and a soldier who practices warfare. There are many other roles that allow the Christian to truly become all things to all men. The Christian's life, therefore, is a mastery of almost all occupations, making a believer a literal jack-of-all-trades and a master of many.

all to the good

> And we know that **all things work together for good** to them that love God, to them who are the called according to _his_ purpose. (Romans 8:28)

Everybody's heard the advice that "Everything will work out for the better." Once again, this expression is true only if that person is a believer according to the verse of scripture above—"to them that love God." Unbelievers who claim this promise are deceiving themselves and others.

This expression is usually spoken when something awful has happened and someone is trying to comfort himself or others.

The next time you hear this phrase used, you might want to tell that person that things aren't going to work out for him if he's not a Christian. Of course, you'll then be bombarded with how judgmental you are. That's when the believer needs to remind this person that Paul prayed that our love "may abound yet more and more in knowledge and *in* all judgment" (Phillipians 1:9).

apple of one's eye

He found him in a desert land, and in the waste howling wilderness; he led him about, he instructed him, he kept him as **the apple of his eye**. (Deuteronomy 32:10)

Moses described God's feelings about Israel in the book of Deuteronomy as "the apple of his eye." Anything or anyone that is considered dear to another is termed the "apple of one's eye." God considered Israel dear to him, not because Israel was better than the other nations, but, as God said, to fulfill his plan for the redemption of mankind. This plan was promised to Abraham and his descendants, which is Israel.

Jews like to brag about being the chosen people (see "chosen people"), but they must remember that God could have chosen any nation to carry out his plan. Another reason God chose Israel was to confound the wise with the fact that a tiny nation such as Israel could play such a major part in the history and future of the world. Just witness the entire Mideast crisis, and you will see that it all revolves around who will control the small Jewish city of Jerusalem—the Muslims, the Jews, or the Christians. It is no accident that Jerusalem has been center stage in world history, and according to Revelation, it will again. Stay tuned.

as good as dead

> Therefore sprang there even of one, and him **as good as dead**, *so many* as the stars of the sky in multitude, and as the sand which is by the sea shore innumerable. (Hebrews 11:12)

God promised Abraham, the patriarch of Israel, that from his seed would come the Messiah, the savior of the world. Abraham had reached 100 years of age, but he and Sarah were still childless. God then decided to give Sarah a child when she "received strength to conceive seed" (Hebrews 11:11). One hundred-year-old people having babies today would be quite a spectacle.

This story foreshadowed the miracle birth of Jesus Christ, who, of course, had the miraculous virgin birth from Mary. To be "as good as dead" is to be under the same conditions as death or similar to them. The birth of Abraham and Sarah's child Isaac also showed how God likes to bring life out of death, thereby teaching us the principle of life after death.

(ashes to ashes), dust to dust

> In the sweat of thy face shalt thou eat bread, till thou return unto the ground; for out of it wast thou taken: for **dust** thou *art*, and un**to dust** shalt thou return. (Genesis 3:19)

As a result of Adam's disobedience in the garden, God cursed man with physical death and strenuous labor, neither of which existed at that time according to Genesis. Since God created man out of dust, death would result in man going back to dust. Yes, man is made of dirt (We have the same elements in our bodies as any sample of common dirt. Isn't that strange?), but combined with God's breath of life, we become a living being. Calling someone a "dirt bag" is quite scriptural—just make sure you explain yourself.

at death's door

Have the gates of death been opened unto thee? or hast thou seen the **doors** of the shadow **of death**? (Job 38:17)

We use the saying "at death's door" to speak of someone about to die. In the midst of Job's suffering and complaints, God answered him with a series of questions, one of which was "...hast thou seen the doors of the shadow of death?" Just like there are literal gates of pearl, or pearly gates, there are also the gates of hell, which are the doors of death. To say someone is "at death's door" is not only speaking of eminent death, but also eminent damnation. When speaking of someone's impending death, it's always better for that person to be at the pearly gates than death's door.

In addition, these doors have locks and keys according to Revelation 1:18 where Jesus says, I "have the keys of hell and death." These same keys were given to the angel in Revelation who opened the "bottomless pit" (another expression and reference to hell).

at peace with the world

When a man's ways please the LORD, he maketh even his enemies to be **at peace with** him. (Proverbs 16:7)

Since the enemies of God are considered "the world," when God's people are at peace with them, they are said to be "at peace with the world." What's interesting here is the fact that God is the one said to make enemies at peace with his children. An unbelieving enemy may not realize why he seems compelled to make peace with a Christian, but that's what happens because of God's intervention.

"At peace with the world" signifies that someone has reached a point where he no longer struggles with the conflicts that come from various people or ideas that he encounters daily. Biblically speaking, this expression does not mean that the Christian won't have enemies, but that his enemies will be forced by God to be at peace with him. If someone who doesn't particularly like you says, "I don't know why I'm doing this for you," you'll already know why.

at your wit's end

> They reel to and fro, and stagger like a drunken man, and are **at their wit's end**. (Psalm 107:27)

A stark picture of God's view of the heathen is shown here in the book of Psalms. God compared the lost to "a drunken man" and to a ship in a stormy sea, and he said they would call on him when they reach "their wit's end." What an indictment of human nature that comment is! Man will only seek God when he has reached his wit's end, or the point of absolute desperation.

It is only when man has exhausted his own "wits" that he comes to God. That is a good thing, for our "wits" can't save us. Our knowledge is not sufficient to reach him. We must all reach our wit's end and rely on his wits if we truly seek to be saved. Needless to say, God's wits don't have an end.

B

baptism of fire

> I indeed baptize you with water unto repentance: but he that cometh after me is mightier than I, whose shoes I am not worthy to bear: he shall **baptize** you with the Holy Ghost, and ***with* fire**: (Matthew 3:11)

Religious people talk today of being "baptized with the Holy Ghost and fire," not realizing that to be "baptized with fire" means to go to hell. The next verse proves this assertion by stating that "he will burn up the chaff with unquenchable fire." The chaff is described in other references as the lost.

Secular people use this phrase to refer to someone being thrown into the middle of a task for the first time and experiencing all the suffering that goes with it. The secular crowd is closer to the real definition than the religious leaders. The next time some "Christian" comes up and says you can receive the baptism of the Holy Ghost and fire, just ask him why he wants you to go to hell.

be about your business

> And he said unto them, How is it that ye sought me? wist ye not that I must **be about my** Father's **business**? (Luke 2:49)

Mary and Joseph were looking for Jesus and found him in the temple. The twelve-year-old so amazed the doctors and priests in the temple that the Bible said they were "astonished at his understanding and answers" (Luke 2:47). Jesus was already the boy wonder just going about his business, his strange business.

People will tell you to go about your business if you're bothering them, but if they tell a Christian that is bothering them the same thing, they must realize that a Christian's business is to preach the gospel, and that in itself bothers a lot of people.

be of good cheer

These things have I spoken unto you, that in me ye might have peace. In the world ye shall have tribulation: but **be of good cheer**; I have overcome the world. (John 16:33)

Jesus Christ is the only man to have ever overcome every temptation put against him, and when his spirit dwells in us, and we yield to it, we can be of good cheer because we now have the power to overcome these temptations also. The "Don't worry, be happy" crowd should be very worried and very unhappy. They are rejecting the only person that can give them happiness.

beat the air

I therefore so run, not as uncertainly; so fight I, not as one that **beateth the air**: (1 Corinthians 9:26)

Other expressions similar to "beating the air" include "spinning your wheels" and "banging your head against a wall." The unbeliever is alluded to as "beating the air" because he doesn't know his true purpose in life or how to obtain it. He is in the proverbial "rat race" and is running in circles. Conversely, the Christian knows the meaning and purpose of life through this one verse: "I am the way, the truth, and the life." Those nine words can stop you in a hurry from "spinning your wheels," "banging your head against a wall," and "beating the air."

become a byword

And thou shalt **become** an astonishment, a proverb, and **a byword**, among all nations whither the LORD shall lead thee. (Deuteronomy 28:37)

God served warning on Israel that if they refused to walk according to his laws, he would curse everything to do with them. "Cursed *shalt* thou *be* when thou comest in, and cursed *shalt* thou *be* when thou goest out" (Deut. 28:19). God gave the law to Israel, not to see if they could keep it, but to show them that they couldn't because of their inherent sinfulness.

What Israel failed to recognize, and what man today also fails to recognize, is that only one person could keep the law without ever breaking it. Perfection is the only standard God will accept, and anybody who thinks he is pleasing God with good deeds apart from faith will receive the same curses as those of Israel.

God doesn't weigh your good deeds against your bad, and even if he did, everyone would fail that test as well. To "become a byword" means the same as it did in biblical days—to be notorious or infamous, just like Israel after God got through dealing with them.

bent out of shape

> For we would not, brethren, have you ignorant of our trouble which came to us in Asia, that we were **pressed** **out of measure**, above strength, insomuch that we despaired even of life: (2 Corinthians 1:8)

"Pressed out of measure's" modern equivalent, "bent out of shape," has changed slightly from its biblical meaning of being pushed to the limit, referring now to someone who gets upset over a matter rather easily. The apostle Paul was so pressed out of measure that he said he "despaired even of life." Yes, even the great Paul had contemplations of wanting to die.

Suicide was not the answer, even though Paul said he had a "desire to depart, and to be with Christ; which is far better. Nevertheless to abide in the flesh *is* more needful for you." (Phillipians 1:23-4). Suicide cults obviously ignore this last verse.

beside yourself

> And when his friends heard *of it*, they went out to lay hold on him: for they said, He is **beside himself**. (Mark 3:21)

Jesus was falsely accused of many things in his day, one of which was being crazy. This accusation came from his "friends" who wanted to apprehend him. In Mark chapter three, Jesus was healing the sick and casting out unclean spirits, actions that were upsetting the establishment of that day, and this caused the Pharisees to believe that he was beside himself, i.e., crazy.

Today, if we claim someone is demon-possessed, we might get that same response. We have other "terms" for people that foam at the mouth and do bizarre things. We lock them up in hospitals, not realizing that what we might be dealing with is no different than it was in Jesus' day— possession of the Devil.

There are many cases of so-called insane people having supernatural strength and doing things that can't be explained medically. We're willing to explain it away as anything but demon possession, and we like to joke about something "possessing" us to do something, but nothing else can explain the absolute madness of some people.

bid someone Godspeed

> Whosoever transgresseth and abideth not in the doctrine of Christ, hath not God. He that abideth in the doctrine of Christ, he hath both the Father and the Son. If there come any unto you, and bring not this doctrine, receive him not into *your* house, neither **bid him God speed**: For he that biddeth him God speed is partaker of his evil deeds. (2 John 9-11)

A careful reading of these verses would shock most people, for they fly in the face of what is taught even by the Christian establishment, and certainly the secular world. First off, having Jesus Christ *is* having the Father and the Son.

Secondly, you are commanded not to let people into your home who believe differently. It doesn't matter even though you're trying to win them to Christ. Thirdly, we are commanded not to wish these people Godspeed, which is to wish them God's blessings, in other words, to wish them well. God does not want us to wish the heathen to have a good day. To do so, he says, makes us a participant of their "evil deeds." You better be careful whom you tell to have a good day because you just have could have ruined yours.

bitter end

> For the lips of a strange woman drop *as* an honeycomb, and her mouth *is* smoother than oil: But her **end is bitter** as wormwood, sharp as a twoedged sword. (Proverbs 5:3-4)

The Bible describes the ramifications of casual sex in a conversation that Solomon had with his son about a promiscuous woman. Solomon warns us of the whorish woman, saying that she talks sweet as honey, but "her end is bitter as wormwood." She is also described as a "twoedged sword," another biblical expression referred to later in this work.

People engaged in casual sex in scripture are not deemed as "fooling around" or having "affairs," but are labeled as "whores" (see Ezekiel 16:33; Proverbs 6:26; Revelation 21:8 etc.). The Bible tells it like it is, and this upsets those people whom it affects, so much so that bibles are changed because of these very terms like "whores," "bastards," etc.

The King James Bible is constantly watered down because of its offensiveness to those who don't like the fact that God himself talks in this manner. Those who feel this way will themselves experience a "bitter end," a rather unpleasant and hard conclusion to a struggle they're in.

blind leading the blind

> Let them alone: they be blind leaders of the blind. And if the **blind lead the blind**, both shall fall into the ditch. (Matthew 15:14)

One of the most popular of all biblical clichés is this one that Jesus used to characterize the Pharisees, the religious leaders of his day. After being informed that the Pharisees were offended at him, Jesus told his disciples that these hypocrites were "blind leaders of the blind," and that they would end up in the ditch. When Jesus called them "blind," he was teaching that they were spiritually blind, i.e., lost sinners, and not only they, but also their followers. You can't cure blindness by pretending to see, and the same applies spiritually.

The situation is no different today, just the names of the organizations have changed. If you want to pattern your life after Jesus, you should expect to have the same confrontations and the same enemies as he. We would never seek directions from a physically blind person, so why do so many seek guidance from the spiritually blind? The answer may be that if you're physically blind, there's no way you can absolutely know if someone else is also. The same holds true in the spiritual realm, and that's why we need Jesus, who makes the blind to see.

bottomless pit

> And the fifth angel sounded, and I saw a star fall from heaven unto the earth: and to him was given the key of the **bottomless pit**. (Revelation 9:1)

Here is an expression that has completely changed in meaning from its original biblical usage. According to Revelation, the "bottomless pit" is the place inside of the earth filled with smoke and locusts—undoubtedly an allusion to hell or the lake of fire.

An interesting side note is that hell is literally a "bottomless pit." Since hell is in the middle of the earth, there would be no gravity there according to scientists. It would be just like floating in space; hence, sinners will be floating in a bottomless pit (i.e., no bottom), and they would have no bearings.

The world, however, has taken this phrase and obscured its intended meaning to now refer to a person who can eat and eat and never get full.

breach of promise

> And the number of the days in which ye searched the land, *even* forty days, each day for a year, shall ye bear your iniquities, *even* forty years, and ye shall know my **breach of promise**. (Numbers 14:34)

As used today, this adage denotes someone who breaks his word with another party. As God used it, he spoke of his promise made to Israel about them inheriting the land. Fulfillment of this promise would be delayed because of Israel's constant complaining of there being "giants in the land" (see also "giants in the land").

You'd probably be a little apprehensive also if you had just seen nine and ten-foot people who didn't want you around. Yes, there were giants in the Bible, and there is ample evidence outside the scriptures that they existed.

The Bible also mentions "monsters" and "dragons," and if you think these are just exaggerations or figurative speech, you ought to read your Bible more carefully. They're not. It is correct, then, to say that Christians believe in giants, monsters, ghosts, devils, talking snakes, and many other so-called fairy tales (see "give up the ghost"). God tests our faith and fear of man with these type beliefs.

break bread

> And upon the first *day* of the week, when the disciples came together to **break bread**, Paul preached unto them, ready to depart on the morrow; and continued his speech until midnight. (Acts 20:7)

Sharing a meal together is the equivalent of "breaking bread," and this phrase is usually used between close friends as it was with Paul and his disciples. Jesus spoke of himself as the "bread of life," and in the same discourse in John chapter six, he said, "Whoso eateth my flesh, and drinketh my blood, hath eternal life; and I will raise him up at the last day" (John 6:54).

Some take this to mean that Christians actually eat the body of Jesus when they take communion with the Eucharist wafers. If this were true, Jesus would be advocating cannibalism, which he, of course, does not. A person can eat a million of these wafers over the course of his life, and it will get him about as much eternal life as he started with—none.

Eternal life, ironically, *is* connected with eating. What does it mean, then, to eat his flesh, since this teaching is connected to eternal life? John 6:63 is the answer, and it connects the disciples' misunderstanding of Jesus' command to eat his flesh to Jesus' own interpretation of what he meant. Jesus said, "It is the spirit that quickeneth; the flesh profiteth nothing: the words that I speak unto you, they are spirit and they are life." The flesh he talked about eating was his *words*, of which we symbolically eat when we believe them as it is stated in Jeremiah 15:16: "Thy words were found, and I did eat them."

break of day

> When he therefore was come up again, and had broken bread, and eaten, and talked a long while, even till **break of day**, so he departed. (Acts 20:11)

Also referred to as "daybreak," "crack of dawn," etc., this idiom was used similarly in the book of Acts. Paul almost literally talked to death a man who was listening to him preach. This man was up on the loft where Paul was preaching and got so tired he fell and nearly died. Paul had been preaching all night and into the morning hours (the "break of day").

People sure seem to get sleepy during sermons, but when's the last time you heard all-night preaching? It was nothing unusual in the early church. America likes its sermons about twenty minutes long with lots of jokes and stories and a scripture every now and then that's not offensive. Microwave Christianity—just add water and mix.

break your heart

> Then Paul answered, What mean ye to weep and to **break mine heart**? for I am ready not to be bound only, but also to die at Jerusalem for the name of the Lord Jesus. (Acts 21:13)

Paul's heart was broken after hearing that his disciples cried. They cried because they didn't want him to go to Jerusalem, for they feared the Jews would apprehend and put Paul in jail as they had before.

A broken heart is precisely what God uses to create a new heart. God has been giving heart transplants longer than any doctor, and he will give anybody one that recognizes that his first heart is evil. As Jeremiah states, "The heart *is* deceitful above all *things*, and desperately wicked: who can know it?" (Jeremiah 17:10). We all are born with a heart condition, but cutting cholesterol won't help this one.

breathe new life into something

> And the LORD God formed man *of* the dust of the ground, and **breathed into** his nostrils the breath of **life**; and man became a living soul. (Genesis 2:7)

An accurate description of how Jesus created man is depicted here as God actually did breathe life into Adam. Please observe that no mention here is made of lightning striking a puddle of organic goop and turning into a frog.

Today, when we speak of "breathing new life" into something, we mean that we're taking something that is old or worn out and reviving it. The use of this phrase "breathe new life" is action that only God could do, so it smacks of blasphemy to attribute this ability to man unless this expression is used in a figurative way.

We should always refrain from taking the unique characteristics of God and placing them on man. For example, it is wrong to say that man is "creative," for man creates nothing if we stick to the definition of "create" which means to "bring into existence out of nothing." Man can no more create anything than he can sprout wings and fly.

bring someone's head on a platter

And **brought his head in a charger**, and gave it to the damsel: and the damsel gave it to her mother. (Mark 6:28)

If someone threatens to "bring your head on a platter," you know you messed up pretty badly. This story in the Bible refers to King Herod's birthday party when the King told his daughter he would give her anything she desired. After the daughter consulted with her mother, both agreed that they wanted the head of John the Baptist on a platter. Herod had already promised her he would give her any request, so he honored it and had John beheaded.

What a testament to the influence of John the Baptist that the King's daughter could have had half her father's kingdom and she instead chose the death of this great man. What an indictment of the wicked also when their conscience won't allow them to let a man of God live. Birthday parties in scripture weren't exactly "pin the tail on the donkey."

bring to light

Therefore judge nothing before the time, until the Lord come, who both will **bring to light** the hidden things of darkness, and will make manifest the counsels of the hearts: and then shall every man have praise of God. (1 Corinthians 4:5)

Any matter that will be brought to light means that all aspects of it will be brought under close scrutiny and revealed. Not only will the unbeliever be judged for his evil deeds, every one of his iniquities will be revealed to everyone else at the Judgment, including his thoughts. What a humiliating and frightening time that will be for the sinner!

The world itself acknowledges this event when it uses the expression "It'll all come out in the wash." Jesus also verified this coming day and said, "Fear them not therefore: for there is nothing covered, that shall not be revealed; and hid, that shall not be known" (Matthew 10:26). There are some who are exempt from this Judgment. If you want an exemption, you will have to apply for exclusive membership to the "Saints of God" club.

bring me word

And he sent them to Bethlehem, and said, Go and search diligently for the young child; and when ye have found *him*, **bring me word** again, that I may come and worship him also. (Matthew 2:8)

To bring word to someone is to deliver a message. Under the pretense of worshipping the child, King Herod wanted to find Jesus, but his real desire was to kill him. The wise men from the East agreed to tell Herod when they found Jesus, not knowing his plans. The wise men weren't as wise as they were cracked up to be.

Incidentally, the scriptures don't say if there were *three* wise men. Herod wanted these wise men to bring him word, but what he really needed was for them to bring him "the Word," one of the names Jesus is called in the book of John.

brother's keeper

And the LORD said unto Cain, Where *is* Abel thy brother? And he said, I know not: *Am* I **my brother's keeper**? (Genesis 4:9)

The inevitable question asked by all big brothers, "Am I my brother's keeper?" was asked by Cain out of jealousy of his brother Abel. Cain and Abel both offered sacrifices to God, but God approved only of Abel's because Abel's was a blood sacrifice and Cain's wasn't. That's where the expression "You can't get blood out of a turnip" might have originated also. You can't get a blood sacrifice out of a vegetable (a turnip). Cain knew that his own offering was wrong, so he tried to substitute his own brand of religion which God rejected.

This whole story exemplifies the futile attempts of any man who tries to come to God without accepting the ultimate blood sacrifice of God's own death on the cross. Anything else is a false, man-made religion that puts you in the same league as Cain, and we are to be "Not as Cain," whom the Bible says "was of that wicked one, and slew his brother. And wherefore slew he him? Because his own works were evil, and his brother's righteous." "Raising Cain" just might be a reference to the attempt of some to "raise" their own religion before God.

build on sand

And every one that heareth these sayings of mine, and doeth them not, shall be likened unto a foolish man, which **built** his house **upon the sand**: And the rain descended, and the floods came and the winds blew, and beat upon that house; and it fell: and great was the fall of it. (Matthew 7:26-7)

Does this story sound familiar? Everyone remembers "The Three Little Pigs" that the wolf was chasing and how the wolf huffed and puffed and blew down two of the pigs' houses that were made of straw and wood. The wolf couldn't blow down the pig's house made of brick, just as the wind couldn't blow down the house built on the rock in Jesus' story.

The Bible shows up in the most unexpected of places, and we use its phrase "built on sand" to denote something that won't last. Nobody with any sense builds a house on sand, so why do we build our spiritual houses on them?

by and by

Yet hath he not root in himself, but dureth for a while: for when tribulation or persecution ariseth because of the word, **by and by** he is offended. (Matthew 13:21)

In Jesus' parable of the sower, the sower plants four kinds of seeds, three of which bear no fruit and one that does. One of the seeds, interpreted as a person's heart, doesn't endure and is offended at the words of the Bible as it is stated in Matthew above.

One of the signs, then, of a wicked heart is a person that is offended at what Jesus calls "the word," or the scriptures. This offense can take on many forms, one of which includes casting doubt on the authenticity of the Bible. An example of this would be someone saying, "A better translation would be..." Belittling the accuracy of certain passages or words with statements such as "This passage really doesn't say this; it really means this or should say this" is another example still.

Some, as mentioned earlier in this work, are offended at the language that the King James uses, that, in their opinion, doesn't sound too nice. The false prophets mentioned in the book of Isaiah agreed with this attitude toward God's words: "Prophesy not unto us right things, speak unto us smooth things, prophesy deceits" (Isaiah 30:10). If you don't like a book that calls a spade a spade, you better stay away from the King James Bible. It's a fistful of reality that will hit you square in the face.

by the letter

And shall not uncircumcision which is by nature, if it fulfil the law, judge thee, who **by the letter** and circumcision dost transgress the law? (Romans 2:27)

When you're a stickler for the rules, you're also said to "go by the book," or "by the letter" as it reads in Romans. Paul was chastising the Jews who wanted to keep the practice of circumcision as a part of the requirements for salvation. He told them that salvation was a matter of circumcising your heart, not your penis, or "privy member," as it is called in the Bible.

Spiritually speaking, circumcision was given by God as a token of the covenant between God and Abraham, but physically applied, circumcision keeps out infections that the uncircumcised may get from time to time.

The Great Physician knows what is best for us, spiritually and physically. David mentioned Goliath the giant's lack of circumcision, not because he cared about the giant's physical condition, but because he wanted to practice the fine art of Christian name-calling; thus, he labeled Goliath an "uncircumcised Philistine."

by the skin of your teeth

My bone cleaveth to my skin and to my flesh, and I am escaped **with the skin of my teeth**. (Job 19:20)

Popping up constantly in modern conversation, "by the skin of your teeth" refers to anyone who just barely makes it or escapes in some situation. This phrase is another example of how unaware people are that they quote the scriptures in their everyday speech.

The story of Job tells of him barely escaping the calamities that befell his children. Job, of course, is famous for his patience, and his story is naturally where we get the phrase "the patience of Job."

Job just happens to be the oldest book in the Bible, and it is one of the oldest in the world. Still, it continues to enrich the English language with numerous, colorful expressions such as "make the hair of your neck stand on end," "watch the sparks fly," "drink it like water," and many more. The more outdated the Bible is accused of being, the more it proves its detractors wrong.

by the sweat of your brow

> **In the sweat of thy face** shalt thou eat bread, till thou return unto the ground; for out of it wast thou taken: for dust thou *art*, and unto dust shalt thou return. (Genesis 3:19)

Part of the original curse God placed on Adam was not work, as commonly thought, but strenuous work. Eve's curse also has been misconstrued as being childbearing, but a careful reading of Genesis shows her curse to be pain in childbearing or "sorrow."

Today, women speak of their monthly periods as "the curse." Biblically speaking, this is somewhat correct if you include their monthly pain as preparation for childbearing.

God said that man would have to sweat for a living, and those of us who have cushy office jobs are recognizing that sweat is just what we need to be healthier.

C

call in question

> For we are in danger to be **called in question** for this day's uproar, there being no cause whereby we may give an account of this concourse. (Acts 19:40)

Lawyers often call in question someone whose suspicious actions imply guilt of some kind. We also say a person that committed a wrongdoing has been "called on the carpet."

The town clerk of Ephesus feared the town's idol makers would revolt if Paul's preaching continued because Paul was having such a devastating effect on their selling of idols: Christianity was putting the idol makers out of business.

The book of Revelation mentions that in the last days, the exact opposite would be the case. The modern church would court the idol makers and incorporate their goods in the church itself and "become the habitation of devils, and the hold of every foul spirit, and a cage of every unclean and hateful bird." Revelation goes on to say that "all nations have drunk of the wine of the wrath of her fornication, and the kings of the earth have committed fornication with her, and the merchants of the earth are waxed rich through the abundance of her delicacies" (Revelation 18:2-3). "Mystery Babylon," the false church, would thrive on idols, and the businesses that sold to it and bought from it would profit greatly from her.

Sound like any church system you know? God destroys "Mystery Babylon," and all the merchants of the earth weep, "for no man shall buy their merchandise any more" (Revelation 18:1-24). Part of its merchandise was the "souls of men" (verse 13), for "by thy sorceries were all nations deceived. And in her was found the blood of prophets, and of saints, and of all that were slain upon the earth" (verse 24).

The ecumenical movement today that is uniting all churches under one banner fits this description perfectly. They claim we all worship the same God whether we be Jew, Muslim, Catholic, Hindu or New Age. What they are saying is true in one sense, for the god they do worship is "the god of this world," and not Jesus Christ, who is "God manifest in the flesh" (1 Timothy 3:16) and who shares his glory with no one. What should be "called in question" is anyone who tries to reconcile true Christianity with the ecumenical movement. Jesus as God can not be reconciled to be identical with any other gods, i.e., Jesus is not Buddha, and Jesus is not Allah.

can a leopard change its spots?

> **Can** the Ethiopian **change** his skin, or the **leopard his spots**? *then* may ye also do good, that are accustomed to do evil. (Jeremiah 13:23)

We do have a few Ethiopian-like people trying to literally change their skin color today, but what God was teaching was that man in and of himself could not change his own nature.

Judah and Jerusalem committed so much evil that they were becoming oblivious to the fact that God would punish them. God said they could no more do good than a leopard could "change its spots."

Even though a leopard can't change its spots, a believer can get them changed. A person is said to have "spots" if he's a sinner (2 Peter 2:13), and, of course, a sinner can have all his spots, i.e., sins, removed by the great spot remover himself, Jesus Christ. He leaves no stains.

cast the first stone

> So when they continued asking him, he lifted up himself, and said unto them, He that is without sin among you, let him **first cast a stone** at her. (John 8:7)

"Casting the first stone" alludes to the famous account in the book of John about the woman caught in adultery who was brought to Jesus to see what he would do with her. Jesus' answer in verse seven ended up convicting the Pharisees, the very people that accused her. This woman was "caught in the act" (see phrase "caught in the act") as it says in verse four of this same chapter in John. The biblical punishment for adultery was death by stoning. If that were the punishment today, half our nation would be dead, but then again, no one commits adultery; they just have an "affair," don't they? The seventh commandment does not read, "Thou shalt not have an affair," so feel free to cast the first stone, or attack, this type of lifestyle and language.

clear as day

> And *thine* age shall be **clearer than the noonday**; thou shalt shine forth, thou shalt be as the morning. (Job 11:17)

Job's friend Zophar accused Job of lying about his reasons for persecution. He advised Job to put away his wickedness, and then his age would be "clearer than the noonday," differing from the present meaning of "clear as day" which signifies something that is made very understandable.

It's getting harder to say something is "clear as day" and mean it literally because our days are becoming less clear due to pollution and smog. If you live in Mexico City or Los Angeles, California, nothing is clear as day; it's about as clear as mud.

come short of

> For all have sinned, and **come short of** the glory of God; (Romans 3:23)

If there's one thing you don't want to come short of, that's the glory of God. If you do, that means you aren't going to heaven, for we need his glory to enter into paradise according to I Peter 4:13, 14, and 5:1. "Coming short" in a matter means not quite attaining your goal, and when it comes to salvation, "almost" doesn't cut it. Forgiveness of sins by faith in Jesus is the only way to be saved, and anybody that attempts any other method is called a "thief" by Jesus himself (see John 10:1). Close may count in horseshoes, but it "comes short" with God.

come to pass

> And now I have told you before it **come to pass**, that, when it is **come to pass**, ye might believe. (John 14:29)

One of the distinguishing characteristics of the Bible involves its use of "come to pass" when it's talking about something that happened. Jesus was having a discussion about going "to prepare a place for you" (verse two), and said, "And if I go and prepare a place for you, I will come again and receive you unto myself; that where I am, *there* ye may be also" (verse three).

Many tend to forget that Jesus was also a prophet, and in this statement, he uttered a prophecy concerning what the believers had to look forward to in heaven. There really will be mansions ("In my father's house are many mansions") in heaven, so don't envy those big houses you see right now; they're nothing like what is in store for the children of God. Not only will Christians be living in these, but they will also be part of an actual city called "New Jerusalem" that will literally come down from the sky and be placed on the earth.

Stories like *The Wizard of Oz* probably got their "yellow brick road" idea from the Bible where it mentions the streets of gold (see phrase "streets of gold") that will be a part of the New Jerusalem that descends from heaven. For a blueprint of this city, see Revelation chapter twenty-one.

coming out of your ears (nose)

Ye shall not eat one day, nor two days, nor five days, neither ten days, nor twenty days; *But* even a whole month, until it **come out at your nostrils**, and it be loathsome unto you: because that ye have despised the LORD which *is* among you, and have wept before him, saying, Why came we forth out of Egypt? (Numbers 11:20)

To have an abundance of something or more than you can handle is to have it "coming out of your ears." God didn't take too kindly to Israel complaining about the "manna from heaven" (see biblical expression "manna from heaven") that he was sending them on a daily basis. They wanted "flesh" to eat; therefore, he told them he would give them quail, so much quail that he said it was going to "come out at your nostrils." God was going to make them sick of quail because of their constant griping about the manna. God has a way of giving us what we want and making us realize we really didn't want it to begin with.

This story should serve notice to all you kids out there who are always griping that your mom is making the same thing all the time. Try eating fried chicken and manna for thirty straight days like the Israelites.

count the cost

For which of you, intending to build a tower, sitteth not down first, and **counteth the cost**, whether he have *sufficient* to finish *it*? (Luke 14:28)

Here we have a little business advice offered by the consummate businessman, Jesus Christ. If his advice were followed, we wouldn't have all these expensive building projects that stick the taxpayer with cost overruns and huge amounts of debt.

Just as a businessman has to decide if it is worth the price to begin an endeavor (i.e., "count the cost"), so also does the sinner have to count the cost and think about what it will cost him to follow Jesus. Even though salvation is free, it is at the same time the costliest thing you can obtain, for it requires the death of self, a price only a few are willing to pay.

Every sinner has to decide to lay down his life for Jesus, for "He that findeth his life shall lose it: and he that loseth his life for my sake shall find it" (Matthew 10:39). Those who know the Bible soon discover that Christianity is the exact opposite of what the world teaches.

cross land and sea

> Woe unto you, scribes and Pharisees, hypocrites! for ye **compass sea and land** to make one proselyte, and when he is made, ye make him twofold more the child of hell than yourselves. (Matthew 23:15)

Jesus lashed out at his long-time enemies, the Pharisees, saying they would go to great lengths and do almost anything, i.e., "cross land and sea," to make a convert. In saying that a convert of the Pharisees was a "child of hell," Jesus, in no uncertain terms, was telling the Pharisees to their face that they were lost, and not only lost, but also children of the Devil. Keep in mind that Jesus was telling this to the leaders of the mainline denominations of his day. Jesus' harshest criticism was reserved for religious leaders because these were the people who gave him the most persecution.

Matthew chapter twenty-three shows the loving and caring Jesus calling these leaders "hypocrites," a "child of hell," "blind guides," "fools and blind," "serpents," a "generation of vipers," and "whited sepulchres." He went on to say they were "full of dead men's bones," and "full of hypocrisy and iniquity."

The world (secular and religious) tells you that this kind of name-calling is wrong, but "what saith the scriptures?" If you think name-calling is un-Christian, then why does Jesus himself, along with Paul and many others, engage in this activity? The reason is that it is perfectly righteous to do so when justified. Any other response makes

Jesus a sinner and shows a complete ignorance of the Bible in this matter.

cross to bear

> If any *man* come to me, and hate not his father, and mother, and wife, and children, and brethren, and sisters, yea, and his own life also, he cannot be my disciple. And whosoever doth not **bear his cross**, and come after me, cannot be my disciple. (Luke 14:27)

It's this kind of verse that drives some so-called believers crazy because they can't fathom how Jesus could be advocating hating your parents, children, and wife. As a result, you have many teachers trying to explain it away as Jesus not really meaning what he said here, or they say what Jesus really meant was that if you loved your parents or kids more than him, you were not worthy of him.

It is the word "hate" that causes people problems with this verse. According to them, since Christianity *supposedly* teaches that God doesn't hate anyone, this verse can't mean what it clearly says. "Hate the sin, and love the sinner" is their cry. The truth is, Christianity does teach that God hates, and not just sin, but the *sinner* also.

There are numerous verses showing that God himself hates the sinner, and this teaching will shock those who have been indoctrinated otherwise. A simple reading of the Bible will clear away all these misconceptions: "The foolish shall not stand in thy sight: thou hatest all workers of iniquity" (Psalm 5:5); "For the wicked boasteth of his heart's desire, and blesseth the covetous, *whom* the LORD abhorreth" (Psalm 10:3); "They that are of a froward heart *are* abomination to the LORD: but *such as are* upright in *their* way *are* his delight" (Proverbs 11:20); "Every one *that is* proud in heart *is* an abomination to the LORD" (Proverbs 16:5).

Why then, as it is argued, does God say he "so loved the world" in John 3:16? The answer is that God does love the world, but is not *in love* with the world. He loves the world, not in a relationship, but on account of what he does for them. He feeds them; he provides for them; he even died for them. In this way he "loves" them. That's what is meant by the command, "Love your neighbor as yourself." You are not to be *in love* with them, but to do good unto them, thereby loving them according to Matthew 5:43-4, which states the following: "Ye have heard that it hath been said, Thou shalt love thy neighbor, and hate thine enemy. But I say unto you, Love your enemies, bless them that curse you, do good to them that hate you, and pray for them that despitefully use you, and persecute you." In Deuteronomy 10:18-9, *God's* definition of "love" as relating to the lost is shown: "He doth execute the judgment of the fatherless and widow, and <u>loveth the stranger, in giving him food and raiment. Love ye therefore the stranger</u>: for ye were strangers in the land of Egypt." After espousing a doctrine like this, you better be prepared to fulfill the expression "bear your cross," for you will be crucified by an onslaught of criticism.

Isn't it interesting that Jesus mentioned that we needed to bear the cross immediately after speaking of hating our parents, kids, and spouses? "Bearing the cross" has nothing to do with walking around with a life-size cross as some have done; to the contrary, it refers to enduring the suffering of your beliefs such as the one presently described. Tell someone who is lost that God hates them, and see what kind of reaction you get. If he is truly seeking God and knows that God does in fact hate him, it just might upset him enough to find out why this is so. In finding out, he would learn of his own wickedness and his need for being saved from eternal damnation. Tell him that God loves him, and you tell him a half-truth that will deceive him in to believing that nothing is wrong with his spiritual condition since God loves him anyway.

God, according to the lost, would never send someone to hell whom he loves. The irony of the matter is that they're right. He sends people to hell whom he hates, but whom he showed love to regardless. It is nothing less than a lie to teach that God sends people to hell whom he loves, but if you believe that God doesn't hate anyone, you are forced to accept this fallacy.

crystal clear

> And he carried me away in the spirit to a great and high mountain, and shewed me that great city, the holy Jerusalem, descending out of heaven from God, Having the glory of God; and her light *was* like unto a stone most precious, even like a jasper stone, **clear as crystal**; (Revelation 21:10-11)

When you understand something very well, you are said to be "crystal clear" on the matter. What was described as "clear as crystal" in the scriptures was the river that flowed out of the throne of Jesus in Jerusalem during Jesus' future reign on earth.

The prophet Ezekiel prophesied of this river and said it would cleanse the entire earth, so all you environmentalists needn't worry that we're going to have to colonize other planets because of all our destruction to earth. Jesus will restore our planet and clean up our mess. No mention is made of Jesus placing us on other planets other than the new earth he will create after destroying the old one 1000 years after he returns.

cut down to the ground

> How art thou fallen from heaven, O Lucifer, son of the morning! *how* art thou **cut down to the ground**, which didst weaken the nations! (Isaiah 14:12)

How appropriate that the one "cut down to the ground" in scripture was Lucifer who lost his authority in heaven as a cherubim (angel) because of his rebellion against God. Originally, Lucifer, or Satan as he is better known, was literally "cut down to the ground" because he was in heaven and was cast down to earth. God cast out Lucifer for staging a rebellion and claiming that he would "be like the most High."

Lucifer's pride as a beautiful cherubim is the same pride that is alluded to in the phrase "cut down to the ground." We usually apply this to those whom we feel are too arrogant and who need to be brought down to earth; thus, we imply that they are so full of pride that they are up in the sky somewhere, just like Lucifer.

cut to the quick

> The God of our fathers raised up Jesus, whom ye slew and hanged on a tree. Him hath God exalted with his right hand *to be* a Prince and a Saviour, for to give repentance to Israel, and forgiveness of sins. And we are his witnesses of these things; and *so is* also the Holy Ghost, whom God hath given to them that obey him. ¶ When they heard that, they were **cut to the heart**, and took counsel to slay them. (Acts 5:33)

A Jewish council that included the high priest decided to tell the apostles not to teach in Jesus' name anymore. This same threat is repeated today when people are pressured, either directly or indirectly, to refrain from using the name "Jesus" in school graduations, public prayers, etc. Instead, they are encouraged to use the generic term "God," which pleases just about all religions except atheists and those Christians who would like to hear the name of this mysterious "God."

Peter's reply to these threats was that he "ought to obey God rather than men" (Acts 5:29). This is the correct thing to do when faced with the dilemma of societal and biblical laws that conflict. "Cutting to someone's heart" involves saying things that convicts a person or upsets him emotionally, or as some say, "That hit home."

D

days are numbered

> So teach *us* to **number our days**, that we may apply *our* hearts unto wisdom. (Psalms 90:12)

When David implored God to "teach us to number our days," he wasn't asking for God to help him make a calendar! If an employee hears that his "days are numbered," he better start looking for another job, for he's getting ready to be fired.

The biblical meaning of this expression refers to David's desire for God to teach him to realize that man's time on earth is short and for him to make the best of it for God. The scriptures teach us that we should all be living like each day could be our last. If we actually did number our days and figure out how many months and days we literally have in an average life, it might help us to put our lives in a more eternal perspective.

By the way, the average seventy-five year old will live approximately 27,000 days or 900 months. It wouldn't be a bad idea if we all had a 900-month calendar to number our days and remind ourselves how short life really is.

dead and buried

> Men *and* brethren, let me freely speak unto you of the patriarch David, that he is both **dead and buried**, and his sepulchre is with us unto this day. (Acts 2:29)

Speaking on the day of Pentecost, Peter reminds the people gathered at Jerusalem that David prophesied of Jesus reigning on the throne of Jerusalem and that Jesus would be a descendant of King David who was "dead and buried." Thus, someone that is dead and buried has been dead a considerable amount of time.

Jesus' genealogical line takes up a good bit of the Bible. All those "begats" are there to prove Jesus' claim to the throne of David and to show his real descent from Adam. Those of us working on our own family trees could only hope to do as good a job as the Bible's.

dead to the world

> God forbid. How shall we, that are **dead to sin**, live any longer therein? (Romans 6:2)

To be "dead to the world" is to be fast asleep. The Bible's use of this phrase differs, taking on a more literal interpretation and means someone who is "dead in Christ," thereby being spiritually dead to the things of this world. A Christian who is not "dead to the world" is not a Christian. Becoming a Christian requires one's spiritual death.

A good test to know if you are "dead to the world" is if you still love the things of this world. "If any man love the world, the love of the Father is not in him" (1 John 2:15). This is what is meant by Jesus' saying, "...he that loseth his life for my sake shall find it."

dearly beloved

> **Dearly beloved**, avenge not yourselves, but *rather* give place unto wrath: for it is written, Vengeance *is* mine; I will repay, saith the Lord. (Romans 12:19)

Often heard at funerals by a preacher, "dearly beloved" is used by God to denote Israel and also New Testament saints, both of whom are called God's "dearly beloved."

"Dearly beloved, we are gathered here today" are the last words most of us want to hear, but if it wasn't for the reality of death, how many of us would ever be mindful of God and the things after death? Thank God for death, for, ironically, it reminds us of eternal life. Without the death of God himself and the shedding of his blood, none of us would have eternal life.

den of thieves

¶ And Jesus went into the temple of God, and cast out all them that sold and bought in the temple, and overthrew the tables of the moneychangers, and the seats of them that sold doves, And said unto them, It is written, My house shall be called the house of prayer; but ye have made it a **den of thieves**. (Matthew 21:13-14)

As used today, a "den of thieves" is a place of ill repute. When Jesus said the temple had become a "den of thieves," he was showing us how the church gets corrupted by the buying and selling of merchandise within its own walls.

Is Jesus condemning the buying and selling of items on church grounds? Scripture answers a resounding "Yes." Some will object and try to justify the selling of these items by pointing out that what is being sold at churches are religious books, tapes, and the like. Certainly, they would argue, Jesus would not be against selling these godly helps. To the contrary, when Jesus got angry and overthrew the moneychangers' tables, they too were selling religious items of that day including doves and other things needed for sacrificing. Of course, to stop this practice would cut in to the pocketbook of those who have a monetary interest in this endeavor, and they couldn't have that now, could they? If they are opposed to stopping this practice, just overthrow a few of their tables, and you'll get their attention.

die before your time

Be not over much wicked, neither be thou foolish: why shouldest thou **die before thy time**? (Ecclesiastes 7:17)

Contrary to what many believe, it is possible to die before your time, or even to die after your time, though it is "appointed unto man once to die, and then the judgment."

Yes, we do have an appointment with death, and it is scheduled just as precise as your next doctor's appointment; however, just as the doctor will allow you to change his appointment, so will God allow you to change his. It all depends on your obedience and your fear of him—just ask Hezekiah. God gave him an extra fifteen years because of his prayer (see Isaiah 38:5), so Hezekiah actually died after his time, but because of most people's rebellion, many will die before their time. The adage, "Only the good die young," can be changed with a little righteous living.

do as I say, not as I do

THEN spake Jesus to the multitude, and to his disciples, Saying, The scribes and the Pharisees sit in Moses' seat: All therefore whatsoever they bid you observe, *that* observe and do; but do not ye after their works: for **they say, and do not**.

Some of us "walk the walk," and some of us just "talk the talk," and the Pharisees and Sadducees were a prime example of how to do neither. The Lord warned us of the "leaven of the Pharisees," this leaven being their doctrine and their hypocrisy according to Matthew 16:12 and Luke 12:1. Neither their lifestyles nor their beliefs were godly, even though the Pharisees intimidated others by their show of religion.

Jesus refused to be intimidated, and he told them to their faces that they were children of the Devil. We should treat the modern-day Pharisees just as the Master did and he will be pleased.

do unto others

And as ye would that men should do to you, **do ye also to them** likewise. (Luke 6:31)

One of the most famous of all biblical expressions is this one that is commonly called the "Golden Rule." Many anti-proverbs have spun off of "do unto others" such as "Do unto others before they do unto you," and "He who has the gold makes the rules."

Jesus used this proverb in his Sermon on the Mount preaching. In this discourse, you will find many colorful expressions such as "straight and narrow," "wolf in sheep's clothing," "eye for an eye," and others that are covered in this work.

Even the unbeliever recognizes the truthfulness and practicality of "do unto others," for most everyone agrees that "doing unto others as you would have them do unto you" is a standard act of courtesy and behavior at home, work, or anywhere.

Of course, there are those sadists who would love to inflict pain and abuse on others because they themselves like it. How does the Golden Rule apply to them? It doesn't because they are sinning in the act of and request for abuse. God's laws are in harmony with each other.

drink it like water

How much more abominable and filthy *is* man, which **drinketh iniquity like water**? (Job 15:15)

To "drink something like water" means just what it says—you drink a particular liquid as much or more than you drink water. This expression is often applied to alcoholics, i.e., drunkards, so the biblical context is not far removed when it speaks of those who "drinketh iniquity like water."

Getting drunk is condemned in the Bible, but the drinking of wine is not. Jesus himself drank wine, not grape juice as some contend. How do we know it was not grape juice instead of wine? Jesus was accused of being a "winebibber" (Matthew 11:19), which is someone who gets drunk from wine. Obviously, you don't get drunk from grape juice, so accusations of drinking grape juice don't make sense.

There are several other instances in scripture that teach that wine drinking is allowed, even recommended: "¶ Go thy way, eat thy bread with joy, and drink thy wine with a merry heart; for God now accepteth thy works" (Ecclesiastes 9:7); "Likewise *must* the deacons *be* grave, not double-tongued, not given to <u>much wine</u>, not greedy of filthy lucre" (1 Timothy 3:8). If even church deacons are not to drink "much wine," that means they can drink some, obviously. Paul admonished the older women in the church "that they be in behaviour as becometh holiness, not false accusers, not given to much wine, teachers of good things;" (Titus 2:3). If "wine" means grape juice, for Paul to admonish the women not to drink much grape juice doesn't even make sense unless "wine" includes the element of alcohol.

drop in the bucket

> Behold, the nations *are* as a **drop of a bucket**, and are counted as the small dust of the balance: behold, he taketh up the isles as a very little thing. (Isaiah 40:15)

Historians like to call attention to the grandeur of empires and nations that have ruled the world at various times, but the one historian that has seen them all, i.e., God, said these nations are to him as "a very little thing."

That ought to go over real well in a United Nations meeting. Compared to God's greatness, these "mighty" nations are a "drop in the bucket," meaning an insignificant amount compared to the whole. Seeing things through God's eyes has a way of helping you see the big picture.

E

earthshaking

> Which **shaketh the earth** out of her place, and the pillars thereof tremble. (Job 9:6)

The only thing said to be earthshaking in the Bible is the earth itself at the hands of God who will shake it in the last days. Job describes God's greatness and might to his friend Bildad the Shuhite and mentions that the earth's pillars tremble, thereby affirming that the earth has pillars that God has set in it.

The phrase "earthshaking" is usually rendered as "It's not earthshaking," meaning there's nothing that's causing any great commotion. As Jerry Lee Lewis sang, and as God promised, there will very soon be "a whole lotta shakin' goin' on."

One of the signs Jesus said would occur in the last days would be the predominance of earthquakes "in divers places." We have had more earthquakes in the last few years than at anytime since man first started recording them. The greatest earthquake in history will actually be in the future. The book of Revelation chapter sixteen prophesies that a great earthquake will devastate the earth just before the return of Jesus Christ. That ought to shake you up a little.

eat, drink, and be merry

> And I will say to my soul, Soul, thou hast much goods laid up for many years; take thine ease, **eat, drink, _and_ be merry**. (Luke 12:19)

The reigning philosophy of the heathen is exemplified in this very popular expression whose modern counterpart is "sex, drugs, and rock-n-roll." The biblical context involves the parable of the rich man who had to build bigger barns to store his goods, and after doing so, decided it was time to relax and "eat, drink, and be merry."

Being happy or merry is the purpose of life for millions including those who profess to know Jesus, but to the knowledgeable Christian, being happy is not, nor should be, his goal. Glorifying God and pleasing him is the purpose for our creation according to Revelation 4:11. As every Christian knows, happiness comes as a result of pleasing God anyway.

eat one's words

Thy **words** were found, and I did **eat them**; and thy word was unto me the joy and rejoicing of mine heart: for I am called by thy name, O LORD God of hosts. (Jeremiah 15:16)

When you make a statement to others that you might regret later, you might have to "eat your words." As far as God is concerned, he would love for you to eat his words, for he says that his words are "sweeter than honey, and the honeycomb."

"O taste and see that the LORD *is* good," said David, as he meditated on the word of God. In fact, God's words are more necessary for us than food itself according to Job 23:12: "I have esteemed the words of his mouth more than my necessary *food*." You won't have to worry about dieting when you eat his words—they're all good for you in any amount.

eats me up

For the zeal of thine house hath **eaten me up**; and the reproaches of them that reproached thee are fallen upon me. (Psalm 69:9)

David prophesied of Jesus' ministry on earth and how the Lord felt about it. What ate Jesus up inside was the zeal that he had for the house of God.

Being called a "zealot" these days carries with it negative connotations; nonetheless, Jesus would be rightfully considered a "zealot" as well as anyone else who has a great zeal for God.

A modern equivalent of the word "zealot" would be "fanatic." Of course, the world seems to think it is okay to be a fanatic about anything except God, or you're labeled a "religious fanatic" and seen as some type of "extremist," another term that is thrown around by people who want you to be a "middle-of-the-roader." Stay in the middle of the road and you'll get run over. If anyone were ever considered an "extremist," it would have to be Jesus Christ, our example.

eleventh hour

And when they came that were hired about **the eleventh hour**, they received every man a penny. (Matthew 20:9)

"The eleventh hour" signifies the time that is left just before a deadline. Jesus applied the term in his parable of the laborers by telling of "eleventh hour" or last minute laborers who were hired by a farmer but who were paid the same wages as the previous helpers that had been there longer.

Since the workers worked a twelve-hour day, it can be assumed this was the normal practice back then as opposed to our eight-hour day today. You even hear talk of Americans switching to a thirty-two hour workweek with a three-day weekend. Scripture says that we should work six days a week and rest on the seventh: "Six days shalt thou labour, and do all thy work" (Exodus 20:11).

There is no such thing as a "weekend" in scripture, and for us to have one each week shows how much we have deviated from the scriptural norm. On the other hand, there are those workaholics who work seven days a week and disobey the commandment to rest on the seventh day (Exodus 20:11).

God knows what is best for us, and he knows that if we don't get our rest, we will have health problems. If we get too much rest, we will have spiritual problems. Working six days a week is the solution that God has commanded.

end is near

They hunt our steps, that we cannot go in our streets: our **end is near**, our days are fulfilled; for our end is come. (Lamentations 4:18)

Just the mention of this phrase conjures up images of the proverbial man with the sandwich boards walking down the street with the words "The end is near" on his front and backside.

As used in the Bible, "The end is near" refers to Israel's complaining of her enemies and her fear that the nation itself was in jeopardy. It's not hard to see the signs of the times (see phrase "signs of the times") and know that "the end is near," the phrase itself being an allusion to the Second Coming of Jesus and the end of time. The end may be near, but that just means a new beginning is approaching for the believer, and a terrifying and fearful end is coming for the unbeliever.

One of the benefits of being a Christian is that God has told us what's going to happen ahead of time, so in essence, the Christian can predict the future because he's read and understood the end of the book. The end is definitely near, but that's just the beginning.

end of the world

Teaching them to observe all things whatsoever I have commanded you: and, lo, I am with you alway, *even* unto **the end of the world**. Amen. (Matthew 28:20)

"Hey, it's not the end of the world," people will say, when trying to comfort you or themselves. Of course, when disaster strikes, people tend to think it is the actual end of the world, but that is another popular misconception.

According to scripture, the world will not end until 1000 years after Armageddon and the return of Jesus. At that time, Jesus will make a "new heaven and a new earth" (Revelation 21:1). The Christian never has to worry about atomic bombs, plagues, overpopulation, or anything else destroying the entire planet, for he knows that Jesus will not allow that to happen until he himself destroys the planet and makes a new one for the church.

Protecting the earth's environment is good, but all the campaigns to "save the planet, save the rain forests," etc., are ignorant of the fact that God will not let them be destroyed in the first place. God's coming back to live on this planet for a thousand years, and afterwards, he will take pleasure in destroying the earth and making a new one.

ends of the earth

> For so hath the Lord commanded us, *saying*, I have set thee to be a light of the Gentiles, that thou shouldest be for salvation unto **the ends of the earth**. (Acts 13:47)

Anyone that will go to great lengths to help you or that will go anywhere to assist you could be described as going to "the ends of the earth" for you. King David says that all people from "the ends of the earth" will come and worship Jesus when he reigns on the earth in the thousand-year reign after his return.

Yes, there will be a thousand-year reign, but not the variety that Hitler talked about. If you're not willing to go to the ends of the earth for Jesus right now, you will be literally forced to do so in the future thousand-year reign when all nations will come and honor the King of Kings, Jesus Christ, once a year from every location on earth. Everyone will literally go to the ends of the earth for Jesus whether they like it or not.

error of one's ways

> Let him know, that he which converteth the sinner from the **error of his way** shall save a soul from death, and shall hide a multitude of sins. (James 5:20)

Those that are humble will say they've seen "the error of their ways" when corrected about any mistaken beliefs they are holding. Turning someone from the error of their ways in the scriptures involves a great deal more than correcting someone's mistaken ideas. It means that you have converted that individual to Christianity.

The next time someone thinks he has been turned from the error of his ways, remind him that for that to happen would require him to be born again. Until that error is corrected, that person will remain in the "error of his ways." Of course, God will be happy to correct that error for you.

evil eye

> Eat thou not the bread of *him that hath* an **evil eye**, neither desire thou his dainty meats: (Proverbs 23:6)

You can always tell the bad guy in the movies—he's the one with the evil eye, i.e., the sinister look. Solomon, the king of Israel, talks about this evil-eyed person in the Proverbs.

It is interesting to note that in the next verse, this person with the evil eye is also the subject of another famous quote: "For as a man thinketh in his heart, so he is." This verse is usually not quoted accurately, for Proverbs 23:7 actually says something quite different: "For as <u>he</u> thinketh in his heart, so is <u>he</u>." The "he" spoken of is the evil-eyed person in the verse above. Scripture does not say, "As a man thinks in his heart so he is." Instead, it says, "he thinketh," speaking of the evil-eyed person just mentioned.

As a result of this correction, the whole philosophy of positive and possibility thinking is shown to be erroneous when it bases itself on this scripture. The eyes tell us a lot about a person, as Jesus himself testified in Matthew 6:22: "The light of the body is the eye: if therefore thine eye be single, thy whole body shall be full of light." Evilness is reflected in the eyes, so don't wonder why some people won't look you in the eye.

eye for an eye

¶ Ye have heard that it hath been said, An **eye for an eye**, and a tooth for a tooth: (Matthew 5:38)

Possibly the best known of biblical expressions is this one that Jesus quotes from the Old Testament. As so often is the case, this scriptural expression is misapplied by most people, and that includes Christians. However, a quick look at the context in Exodus chapter twenty-one would clear up the misinterpretation. "An eye for an eye" was the method a judge would use to determine the proper punishment for a crime; thus, the punishment would fit the crime.

The Bible does not give a Christian license to go around doing the work of a judge. At the same time, a judge is not to circumvent this punishment that God has prescribed by giving lighter sentences, probation, plea-bargaining, and other legal twists. The Bible teaches that if a man murders someone, he should die also. Any other punishment is condoning the murder and rewarding the criminal.

No wonder our crime is rampant in this country. The ironic thing is that this country knows how to drastically reduce crime—it just won't follow the biblical procedures to do so. Why is this the case? The people that run our judicial system feel that people in general are just not as bad as the Bible says they are. According to them, nobody really wants to commit murder, rape, or robbery, for a "good" person is not evil to begin with.

Moreover, according to this philosophy, society is to blame for all of man's evil deeds, not the men themselves; therefore, to punish man is wrong. Now we are told that crime is committed because we have criminal genes that make us this way; thus, people are predisposed to do what they do and have no control over their wills. This is what we've come to—nobody is responsible for anything he does because it's really the fault of society, the environment, or his genes. Of course, that idea is very readily received by those who don't like the fact that God himself is a judge who will punish their sins in the lake of fire. To believe this other psychological nonsense will conveniently allow you to escape the judgment of God, for he surely can't hold you responsible for what society and your genes have done to you, can he? "Be not deceived; God is not mocked: for whatsoever a man soweth, that shall he also reap" (Galatians 6:7).

F

face-to-face

And Jacob called the name of the place Peniel: for I have seen God **face to face**, and my life is preserved. (Genesis 32:30)

Each one of us, like Jacob, will have a face-to-face meeting with the God of this universe, for God says, "that at the name of Jesus every knee should bow" and also "*that* every tongue should confess that Jesus Christ *is* Lord." Your knees will not bow because you are forced to but because of the sheer greatness of Jesus himself will you fall to the ground and worship. It will be like the scarecrow meeting the Wizard of Oz—just multiply that experience times ten-thousand.

We are not meeting some ambiguous spirit; we will actually see the face of God, Jesus Christ, whom it says "...is the image of the invisible God" (Colossians 1:15). When you see Jesus on the throne, don't ask him to give you a new heart like the Wizard did for the tin man—it'll be a little too late.

fall by the wayside

And when he sowed, some *seeds* **fell by the way side**, and the fowls came, and devoured them up: (Matthew 13:4)

In his parable of the sower, Jesus described four kinds of soil that a certain sower planted his seeds in, the seeds being the word of God, and the different soils representing the various hearers of the word. Only one soil ultimately became productive, and three did not. The seed that the Bible says "fell by the wayside" corresponded to the person whom had his seed taken away by Satan for not understanding what was preached to the hearer.

"Falling by the wayside" speaks of something that has gone in to disservice or someone that has just dropped out of society. Spiritually speaking, "falling by the wayside" takes on a far more serious note, signifying the seeds of those who don't get "planted" correctly.

You've got to have the right seed (the word of God) and the right soil (a hungry heart) to produce the right crop (a born-again soul). No Christian ever sprung from any other source, and you definitely won't fool the consummate farmer himself, Jesus Christ, who knows the difference between a tare and a good crop.

fall from grace

Christ is become of no effect unto you, whosoever of you are justified by the law; ye are **fallen from grace**. (Galatians 5:4)

Paul blasts the notion that a Christian has to earn his way to heaven by good works. Christians that believe this, he says, have "fallen from grace," meaning they no longer are living by the grace of God.

Today, this meaning has shifted somewhat to include falling out of favor or losing one's position in any endeavor. You definitely fall out of favor with God if you hold this belief of earning your way to heaven by your good deeds. If you believe God weighs your good and bad and passes judgment accordingly, you miss the whole reason that God had to save man in the first place—because man's evil heart prevents him from saving himself through good works.

God can't be bribed with your good deeds; he only looks for what you believe and if you really believe it. "This is the work of God, that ye believe on him whom he hath sent" (John 6:29). "For he that is entered into his rest, he also hath ceased from his own works, as God did from his" (Hebrews 4:10). You can't buy something that's free from the start, and you can't work for God if he's not hiring.

fall into the hands of ...

It *is* a fearful thing to **fall into the hands of** the living God. (Hebrews 10:31)

Sometimes things are said to have "fallen into the wrong hands" if they end up in the possession of an undesirable person. In the Bible, the only hands anybody or anything falls into are God's, who, unlike the popular commercial, you're not always "in good hands" with. It is a "fearful thing" to fall into God's hands if you are an unbeliever. No insurance company can help you with that.

Even so, God has "the whole world in his hands" as the song says and as Job echoes in Job 12:10: "In whose hand *is* the soul of every thing, and the breath of all mankind." It looks like people are in his hands whether they like it or not.

fall on your sword

And when his armourbearer saw that Saul was dead, he **fell** likewise up**on his sword**, and died with him. (1 Samuel 31:5)

"Shooting yourself in the foot" would be a close equivalent of this biblical expression found in the book of Samuel. This saying is another example of a literal expression of the Bible being turned into a metaphorical one for today.

King Saul committed suicide after realizing that he was going to lose his battle against the Philistines, and upon seeing Saul's demise, his armor bearer did the same. If you fall on your sword, you do yourself more harm than you're able to recover from.

Even though we don't carry swords around anymore, the disciples did, and Jesus approved of it. In fact, he said if you don't have a sword, sell some of your clothes and go buy one: "Then said he unto them, But now, he that hath a purse, let him take *it*, and likewise *his* scrip: and he that hath no sword, let him sell his garment, and <u>buy</u> one" (Luke 22:36).

When's the last time you heard Christians advocating the idea of selling your clothes and buying guns instead? We hear the opposite these days from the anti-gun crusaders who tell people to sell their guns and buy more clothes. Therefore, go buy you a sword, gun, or any other weapon, and don't be talked out of it by those who say Jesus didn't allow for it. Just don't "fall on your sword," and you'll be alright.

far be it from me

> And Joab answered and said, Far be it, **far be it from me**, that I should swallow up or destroy. (2 Samuel 20:20)

An equivalent expression might be, "I wouldn't dream of doing such a thing." Joab, one of David's officers in his army, was pursuing a man named Sheba who took up arms against David. Joab followed him to a certain city and told that city's leader that he wanted only Sheba, not the city. Speaking of the city, he said, "Far be it from me that I should swallow up or destroy."

"Far be it from me" is another example of why the Bible needs no updating; on the contrary, this amazing book constantly updates our language and provides us hundreds of colorful and interesting expressions that have survived the test of time, even after 4,000 years of use. "Far be it from us" to discount the impact this book continues to make on our society.

fear of God, (put the ... into someone)

> And **the fear of God** was on all the kingdoms of *those* countries, when they had heard that the LORD had fought against the enemies of Israel. (2 Chron. 20:29)

It seems that the countries of this world would have learned by now that God definitely does protect Israel and fights against those countries that fight against her. Israel went 2,500 years with God not allowing her to become a country, but he changed everything for his purposes when Israel became a nation again over fifty years ago.

The fact that Israel even exists is a modern miracle. She is surrounded by enemies that have waged war constantly to destroy her, but God has protected her as he promised he would. He has done this by "putting the fear of God" on all those countries who fight and try unsuccessfully to defeat her.

One reason that the United States has always defended Israel could be that its leaders have believed the scriptures that say Israel and its supporters will be protected by God: "And I will bless them that bless thee, and curse him that curseth thee..." (Genesis 12:3).

When someone has "the fear of God" put into him as these countries have, it means that he gets "scared straight" as we say today.

feet of clay

His legs of iron, his **feet** part of iron and part **of clay**. (Daniel 2:33)

When you learn about a particular fault someone has that you didn't suspect he or she had, this person is said to have "feet of clay"—an undetected weakness. As used in the book of Daniel, "feet of clay" made reference to the feet of a person that Daniel saw in a vision.

According to the Bible's own interpretation of the vision, certain parts of the person's body in Daniel's vision each represented kingdoms that were to rule the world. The image's feet stood for the fourth and last kingdom described as "part of iron and part of clay."

Certain commentators say that this can only signify the Roman empire in a new form for the last days before Christ returns. In Europe today, various countries are all slowly uniting their currencies and governments in an attempt to create a United States of Europe out of which will emerge someone who many feel will be the predicted world leader, the Antichrist. He will have an inherent weakness, though, because the image's iron and clay do not mix, possibly showing that he will not have a strong alliance in the long term.

Thus, it can be seen how the idea of weakness came to be associated with the expression "feet of clay." Of course, "feet of clay" can be literally applied to Adam whom God created out of the dust of the ground, that is, clay. His weakness, or feet of clay, however, was his wife, whom he chose to die with instead of obeying God and not eating the forbidden fruit. Man ended up choosing a woman over God himself, a fact that ought to demonstrate the power that women have over men. Man's feet of clay is almost always his woman.

fight like men

> Be strong, and quit yourselves like men, O ye Philistines, that ye be not servants unto the Hebrews, as they have been to you: **quit yourselves like men, and fight**. (1 Samuel 4:9)

In this day of women's rights and the feminist movement, phrases like this don't go over too well with the modern woman. We are never encouraged to "fight like a woman."

The Philistines were battling Israel and exhorted each other to "fight like men" after some of their men had expressed fear on account of how Israel had conquered other armies with the famous Ark of the Covenant. This ark became the subject matter of a modern movie in the *Raiders of the Lost Ark* series.

It must be remembered that the exhortation to "fight like a man" was not given by God but rather by the Philistines. God does exhort us to fight, but to learn about that, see the next passage.

fight the good fight

Fight the good fight of faith, lay hold on eternal life, whereunto thou art also called, and hast professed a good profession before many witnesses. (1 Timothy 6:11)

To "fight the good fight" involves being aggressive in defending a good cause. Paul is reminding his young disciple Timothy that to be a good Christian, Timothy has to be like a soldier in a war because the true Christian is fighting a real war with real enemies.

The Bible teaches us how to love and how to fight. Fortunately, we have the ultimate fighter himself, Jesus Christ, fighting for us. He remains undefeated to this day, having knocked out all "challengers" including his main contender, Satan. Three scriptural blows were all it took (see Matthew chapter four).

filthy lucre (rich)

A bishop then must be blameless, the husband of one wife, vigilant, sober, of good behaviour, given to hospitality, apt to teach; Not given to wine, no striker, not greedy of **filthy lucre**; but patient, not a brawler, not covetous; (1 Timothy 3:3)

"Filthy rich" and "filthy lucre" both refer to money gotten illegally or immorally. In the scriptures, this phrase makes reference to false teachers and preachers who teach "for filthy lucre's sake," i.e., just for the money.

As it states above, one of the qualifications of a bishop is that he can't be greedy of "filthy lucre." This would disqualify many in the church today who spend much of their time begging for money through telethons and donations when the Bible says, "I have never seen the righteous forsaken, nor his seed *begging* for bread."

Many in the church today seem to have compassion for the lost, but a lot of this "compassion" is just a smoke screen for getting more people in the church. Why? More people means more tithes collected and helps to finance everyone's building programs. "The love of money is the root of all evil."

fire and brimstone

> But the fearful, and unbelieving, and the abominable, and murderers, and whoremongers, and sorcerers, and idolaters, and all liars, shall have their part in the lake which burneth with **fire and brimstone**: which is the second death. (Revelation 21:8)

Those who constantly preach on hell and the lake of fire are labeled "fire and brimstone" preachers and are relegated as too harsh and unloving by much of modern man. This criticism would have to be levied upon Jesus, Paul, and the other disciples as well. They were always preaching on hell and damnation.

In Mark chapter nine, Jesus told the same people three times that hell awaited those who rejected God, saying that hell is "where their worm dieth not, and the fire is not quenched." In 2nd Thessalonians chapter one, Paul spoke of God's wrath being poured out on the heathen: "In flaming fire taking vengeance on them that know not God, and that obey not the gospel of our Lord Jesus Christ." There is no symbolism or figurative language here.

fire in his eyes

> His head and *his* hairs *were* white like wool, as white as snow; and his **eyes *were* as a flame of fire**; (Revelation 1:14)

Guess who has fire in his eyes in the Bible? It was the loving, caring Jesus according to the apostle John's vision of Jesus in the book of Revelation. To have "fire in your eyes" means you are extremely angry, and this usage is connected in meaning with the biblical context where Jesus is described as having eyes "as a flame of fire."

It is seldom taught today that God is angry with anyone, but the Bible declares otherwise in Psalms chapter two where it says God "is angry with the wicked every day." Jesus is so angry with the wicked that he will literally kill millions of people at his second coming and will actually crush the wicked like grapes soaking his own garment with their blood (Isaiah 64). There will be so much bloodshed that the blood of the wicked will reach the horses' bridle to a distance of 200 miles (Revelation 14:20). Some commentators contend that the Red Sea was so named because of the blood that will pour into it from this battle.

flesh and blood

> And Jesus answered and said unto him, Blessed art thou Simon Bar-jona: for **flesh and blood** hath not revealed *it* unto thee, but my Father which is in heaven. (Matthew 16:17)

Your own "flesh and blood" is another way of saying your children, parents, relatives, or people in general. Jesus employed the term when asking Peter who men said the Son of Man was. Peter's answer that Jesus was "the Son of the living God" was not revealed to him by "flesh and blood"—in other words, man, but by God himself.

"Whom say ye that I am" is the most important question you'll ever answer about Jesus. The right answer to this question is connected with the "flesh and blood" phrase itself, for God took on flesh and blood by becoming a son. Man never could become God, so God became a man.

fly in the ointment

> Dead **flies** cause **the ointment** of the apothecary to send forth a stinking savour: *so doth* a little folly him that is in reputation for wisdom *and* honour. (Ecclesiastes 10:1)

Just as a fly in the soup ruins a meal, so does a fly in the ointment ruin a jar of Vaseline! As it is used in this verse of scripture, the "fly in the ointment" is ruining a good man's reputation. How is it ruined?—when he commits a "little folly."

A wise man will shun foolishness and folly for this very reason, but there are some who see no harm in a little playfulness and folly. For those who feel this way, Proverbs 26:18-19 should be avoided: "As a mad *man* who casteth firebrands, arrows, and death, So *is* the man *that* deceiveth his neighbor, and saith, Am I not in <u>sport</u>?"

Practical jokers are compared to madmen and deceivers. Doing these things, is, in effect, lying and deceiving. In God's eyes, jokers and kidders are no different than a common liar, and that's no joke.

follow in the steps of...

> For even hereunto were ye called: because Christ also suffered for us, leaving us an example, that ye should **follow his steps**: (1 Peter 2:21)

How appropriate that the person we are to "follow in the footsteps of," or emulate, according to scripture, is Jesus Christ himself. Following anyone else could lead you to idolatry which is masqueraded as heroes and role models today. If you want to play "follow the leader," follow the true one, Jesus Christ, and you will never be disappointed.

for Christ's sake

> We *are* fools **for Christ's sake**, but ye *are* wise in Christ; we *are* weak, but ye *are* strong; ye *are* honorable, but we *are* despised. (1 Corinthians 4:10)

To utter "for Christ's sake" is to implore someone or to express unbelief or amazement. Its usage in the Bible is literal, as opposed to the modern, euphemistic counterpart. "We are fools," Paul said, "for Christ's sake," speaking of the apostles' persecution and their being "appointed to death."

Every time one utters this expression, he is asking for some action to be done on behalf of Christ whether he believes in Christ or not. It's funny how God gets even the unbeliever to acknowledge his need of Jesus.

four corners of the earth

> AND after these things I saw four angels standing on **the four corners of the earth**, holding the four winds of the earth, that the wind should not blow on the earth, nor on the sea, nor on any tree. (Revelation 7:1)

"The four corners of the earth" speaks of far away places as we use it today. Maybe this saying is where some got the notion that the earth is flat; thus, modern man might blame the Bible for fostering incorrect, scientific notions about the earth.

Ah, but if these same doubters would have bothered to look in the book of Isaiah, they would have been startled to see that God "sitteth upon the circle of the earth" (Isaiah 40:22). The fact that the earth is round like a ball was known thousands of years before the scientists claimed to have known it. Reading your King James Bible will always keep you ahead of the pack.

from time to time

> And thy meat which thou shalt eat *shall be* by weight, twenty shekels a day: **from time to time** shalt thou eat it. (Ezekiel 4:10)

God told men to do some strange things in the Bible, and Ezekiel was a prime example. God instructed the prophet to lie on his side 390 consecutive days, each day to represent a year of Israel's iniquity. While lying on his side, Ezekiel was to eat meat and drink "from time to time."

Perhaps the reason he was supposed to eat "from time to time" and not more often was that his food was to be cooked with human dung according to God. God was sending a message to the Israelites about their sinfulness, but poor Ezekiel had to wake up to the sweet aroma of dung-baked breakfast every morning. That gives new meaning to food that tastes like "crap."

fuel to the fire

> Thou shalt be for **fuel to the fire**; thy blood shall be in the midst of the land; thou shalt be no *more* remembered: for I the LORD have spoken *it*. (Ezekiel 21:32)

Don't "add fuel to the fire" we are told when we make a bad situation worse. God prophesies of his judgment of the Ammonites for their lying and vanity against Israel. Because of this, he says that the Ammonites will be "fuel to the fire." All an unbeliever will be good for is fuel to the fire when he is cast into hell, the fire that never runs out of fuel.

G

get your house in order

IN those days was Hezekiah sick unto death. And the prophet Isaiah the son of Amoz came to him, and said unto him, Thus saith the LORD, **Set thine house in order**; for thou shalt die, and not live. (2 Kings 20:1)

God told King Hezekiah to "Set thine house in order" because the king was going to die. God, however, extended his life by adding fifteen years to it on account of the prophet's fervent prayer. We usually hear this expression when something serious is going on and we need to have ourselves prepared and organized.

"Order" ought to be a trademark of a Christian's life. "Out of order" is God's opinion of the way the world operates. Like everything else, the master mechanic can fix it.

give credit where credit is due

Render therefore to all their dues: **tribute to whom tribute *is due***; custom to whom custom; fear to whom fear; honour to whom honour. (Romans 13:7)

When Jesus was asked about paying taxes, his reply was to "Render therefore unto Caesar the things which are Caesar's"—a can't lose slogan for the IRS if there ever was one. Everyone's favorite government agency, the Internal Revenue Service, is more holy and a lot less "infernal" than you think. Need the Bible remind you, they are called God's ministers to whom we are to pay taxes. Of course, if they owe us money, then they need to give credit where credit is due, or as the Bible says, "tribute to whom tribute is due."

Acknowledging someone's accomplishments is the meaning of "giving credit where credit is due." Acknowledging the IRS as God's ministers, though not an easy task, is something that might make it easier to pay those taxes come April 15th. You definitely don't want to owe back taxes to God or his ministers. He and they have a way of retrieving them if you haven't found that out already.

give up the ghost

> Then Abraham **gave up the ghost**, and died in a good old age, an old man, and full *of years*; and was gathered to his people. (Genesis 25:8)

Yes, there are ghosts in the Bible, and, yes, there is a friendly ghost, but it's not Casper; it is the Holy Ghost. "Giving up the ghost" is used in place of saying someone died, and it is also happens to be a more accurate account of what actually occurs at death. When an individual dies, the Bible says the spirit, or ghost, returns "unto God who gave it" (Ecclesiastes 12:7).

Telling children that there are no such things as ghosts is contrary to biblical teaching. While we're on the subject, don't neglect to teach that there are monsters as well—just look in the book of Lamentations. While you're at it, don't forget about the dragons and the "fiery flying serpents" (Isaiah 30:6) mentioned throughout the Bible.

These words seem to embarrass some Bible translators, so they decided to change these terms in the newer versions. A true Christian should have no problem believing that there are monsters in the sea, dragons in the desert (isn't that thing called the Komodo dragon?), and ghosts. We haven't even touched on behemoth or leviathan, the dinosaurs that the Bible says existed at the time of man. Since scientists would have a conniption fit with that concept, the other translations followed suit and removed their references by referring to them as hippopotamuses or alligators, both of which are incorrect translations. If you bother to read the context in the book of Job, you will notice that leviathan can't be anything but a dinosaur (See Job chapter 41). The King James Bible has to qualify as the most insightful, yet most critically attacked book ever written.

gnash your teeth

> But the children of the kingdom shall be cast out into outer darkness: there shall be weeping and **gnashing of teeth**. (Matthew 8:12)

A fitting way to describe anger is this phrase quoted by Jesus who described the feeling that those being cast into hell will experience. The wicked quite often gnash their teeth in scripture, and maybe all this gnashing prompted King David to tell God to "break their teeth" (Psalms 58:6).

Praying for your enemies' teeth to be broken doesn't bode well with most Christians; however, God didn't reprimand David for asking for this supposed reprehensible action. The only reprimand comes from teeth-gnashing "scholars" who deem this verse too harsh to be taken literally. It is not only literal, it is a righteous desire, and that is what causes all the teeth to "gnash" in the first place. Before you scream that it is not right for believers to do these things, notice that God is the one who is supposed to do the breaking of teeth. Take it up with him.

go on all fours

> Whatsoever goeth upon the belly, and whatsoever **goeth upon *all* four**, or whatsoever hath more feet among all creeping things that creep upon the earth, them ye shall not eat for they *are* an abomination. (Leviticus 11:42)

Chocolate covered grasshoppers are a definite no-no for a Jew to eat because they are creeping things that "goeth upon all four." God was telling Moses and Aaron the difference between the clean and unclean things they could eat. To "go on all fours" is to act like an animal. The Jews, as most know, can't eat certain foods like pork, fish with scales, or meat with blood in it. The Jews would probably accuse

John the Baptist of acting like an animal who goes on all fours because he went around eating "locusts and wild honey."

The New Testament allows the Christian to eat these meats and insects if he so chooses: "Let not him that eateth despise him that eateth not; and let not him which eateth not judge him that eateth: for God hath received him" (Romans 14:3). It is not cruel to kill animals and to eat meat no matter what the vegetarians tell you.

go the way of all flesh

> I **go the way of all the earth**: be thou strong therefore, and shew thyself a man; (1 Kings 2:2)

The only sure things according to this world are death and taxes, and for them they are right. The exception to this rule was Enoch and Elijah who escaped death and were taken up into heaven. These two men's departure before death foreshadowed what will happen to the Christians living in the last days who will be taken into heaven and escape death.

For those of us who will die before this event and have to "go the way of all the earth" as stated by King David in this passage, that's life. There are some benefits in being a last-days Christian, but your need for a nice funeral is not one of them.

go to hell

> Let death seize upon them, *and* let them **go** down quick in**to hell**: for wickedness *is* in their dwellings, *and* among them. (Psalms 55:15)

If you feel the urge to utter this to some unsuspecting soul, take comfort in knowing that this action was not condemned by God when King David said this very thing about one of his enemies. Not only was this person David's enemy, he was also a supposed believer who David "walked unto the house of God in company" with.

David was obviously deceived by his friend, and David's reaction of wishing his friend would "go down quick into hell," albeit shocking, is, nonetheless, scripturally sound advice to any of you needing to do the same to others. Just be sure to tell them that you are saying what any Christian ought to tell those who live as though they want to go to hell.

go through fire and water

Thou hast caused men to ride over our heads; we **went through fire and through water**: but thou broughtest us out into a wealthy *place*.   (Psalms 66:12)

A modern rendition would be "go to hell and back" and speaks of going to great lengths and striving diligently for someone or something. The Israelites made reference to this phrase but meant it literally when they mentioned going through the Red Sea's wall of water and the "pillar of fire" that protected them from the Egyptians.

The history of God's judgments on earth can also be summed up as going through fire and water. Noah's flood was the water judgment, and fire is the next: "Whereby the world that then was, being overflowed with water, perished: But the heavens and the earth, which are now, by the same word are kept in store, reserved unto fire against the day of judgment and perdition of ungodly men" (2 Peter 6-7). God has no intention of saving this earth for anyone; he's going to make a new one that's even better.

God bless you

The **Lord bless thee**, and keep thee: (Numbers 6:24)

Just because God blesses you, don't get the notion that all is well. Throughout scripture, God blesses even the heathen (a name intolerant to some, yet biblical to others). As some preachers might say, "God will bless your socks off and send you straight to hell at the same time," and "this witness is true," as the Bible would say.

Even though God does bless us with all his many wonderful things, let us not forget that he also curses those who are against him, and that's not talking about using "bad" language of which there is plenty of that in the King James as well (see "bastard," "teat," "whore," "dung," "piss," "go to hell," "damned," etc.).

God forbid

> What then? shall we sin, because we are not under the law, but under grace? **God forbid**. (Romans 6:15)

Speaking to the church at Rome, Paul tried to dispel the notion that Christians could continue in sin because they weren't "under the law, but under grace." Paul's reaction was a resounding "no," or "God forbid." Paul was not advocating a license to sin, but at the same time, he was not saying our salvation depended on not sinning.

People always ask what a Christian can and can't do and still go to heaven. Once you have believed and been saved, no matter what you do, you will still go to heaven. Does this mean you can do anything? The answer is quite surprising to those who are of little understanding of salvation. Yes, you can do any sin in the book and still go to heaven, for any sin you commit has already been forgiven, and that includes sins in the future. Could you murder, lie, steal, and commit adultery? Yes, you can. Should you or would you?—of course not.

Would a Christian do these things? Just look at the Christians in the Bible who did these things and are in heaven today. Moses and David both murdered. Abraham lied and was a polygamist. Solomon committed idolatry by worshipping his wives' gods. Noah got drunk, and Job cursed God for the day that Job was born. These actions all occurred after they became Christians, and none of these people lost their salvation.

Once you are born again, you can't undo the fact that you are a child of God because you can do nothing to corrupt that part of you that will inherit heaven—the spirit man: "Being born again, not of corruptible seed, but of incorruptible, by the word of God, which liveth, and abideth for ever" (1 Peter 1:23). Man usually manages to screw up just about everything that God has entrusted to him; fortunately, God gave us something that we can't mess up— "incorruptible seed."

God is my witness

> For **God is my witness**, whom I serve with my spirit in the gospel of his Son, that without ceasing I make mention of you always in my prayers; (Romans 1:9)

Anytime you hear that there are no eyewitnesses to a crime, that is not a true statement. There has been an eyewitness to every crime ever committed over the history of time, and that witness is Jesus Christ. Just think if you had access to view every crime committed in every second of every day. God has this access, for "The eyes of the LORD *are* in every place, beholding the evil and the good (Proverbs 15:3). You think you're sick of evil? Try putting yourself in God's place.

God save the king

> And it came to pass, when Hushai the Archite, David's friend, was come unto Absalom, that Hushai said unto Absalom, **God save the king, God save the king**. (2 Samuel 16:16)

No English king is crowned without hearing "God save the king" proclaimed. Hushai, a friend of King David, also proclaimed these very words when he met David's son Absalom. Absalom didn't want God to save the king; instead, he wanted to overthrow his father David.

Like Absalom, we Americans don't take kindly to kings we don't like either, so we took up arms against the one we had which was nothing short of outright rebellion against "the powers that be" (see phrase "powers that be"). This, of course, is rebellion against God himself who sets up these kings to reign over us. You don't read of Jesus telling his disciples to overthrow King Herod, who, by the way, killed John the Baptist and wanted to kill Jesus as well.

Kings around the world don't get the respect and honor they deserve despite the scriptures clear admonitions for their honor: "Fear God. Honour the king (1 Peter 2:17). When the King of kings reigns supreme in Jerusalem, he will get respect, and he will not share any of his power with the Supreme Court or Congress. God doesn't operate his government democratically.

good for nothing

¶ Ye are the salt of the earth: but if the salt have lost his savour, wherewith shall it be salted? it is thenceforth **good for nothing**, but to be cast out, and to be trodden under foot of men. (Matthew 5:13)

Christians should take heed at this warning given by Jesus in his preaching to the multitudes. He stated that if the "salt of the earth," or Christians, "have lost his savour," they have become "good for nothing" and will be "trodden underfoot of men." In other words, if a Christian has lost his testimony or zeal for God, he is not fit to do anything in this world and will end up a reject. He will not be useful for the world, the church, or God; thus, he will be useless, i.e., "good for nothing."

Trying to please the world and God not only is wicked and worthless (good for nothing), but also will get you "trodden under foot of men," or "stepped all over," as the world would say.

good Lord

For a multitude of the people, *even* many of Ephraim, and Manasseh, Issachar, and Zebulun, had not cleansed themselves, yet did they eat the passover otherwise than it was written. But Hezekiah prayed for them, saying, **The good LORD** pardon every one *That* prepareth his heart to seek God, the LORD God of his fathers, though *he be* not *cleansed* according to the purification of the sanctuary. (2 Chronicles 30:18-19)

A common title given to Jesus today is "The Good Lord," an appellation and expression used since the times of King Hezekiah of Israel 2,700 years ago. The use of the term "good" to describe God was discussed by Jesus himself when someone came up to him and called him "Good Master." Jesus asked him why he was calling him "good" when there was only one that is good (God) according to Jesus.

Muslims like to use this verse to show that Jesus was saying he wasn't God, that only God was good, not himself. This verse teaches the very opposite fact. Jesus was saying, in effect, "If you're calling me good, you're calling me God." Jesus never denied he was God; in fact, he proclaimed it over and over again: "Destroy this temple, and in three days I will raise it up...But he spake of the temple of his body." (John 2:19, 21).

Jesus raised his own body from the dead, but the scriptures also say it was God who did it. There is no other way to reconcile those scriptures but to acknowledge that Jesus is the one who raises the dead and also is the one who was raised—God and man in one person. Don't call him good unless you believe he is nothing less than God himself.

good name

A GOOD name *is* rather to be chosen than great riches, *and* loving favour rather than silver and gold. (Proverbs 22:1)

A good name "is better than precious ointment" according to Ecclesiastes 7:1. When a person has a good name in the community, he usually is considered a person of integrity. However, beware "when all men speak well of you," as Jesus said, "for so did the fathers to the false prophets."

Having a good name is not the same as having everyone like you. You should have a good name in the community, but you should also have many enemies if you are living the life of a Christian. Trying to make everyone like you is the job of a politician, not a Christian. A Christian with no enemies is not living for God, just for his supposed good name.

goodness' sake

> Remember not the sins of my youth, nor my transgressions: according to thy mercy remember thou me **for thy goodness' sake**, O LORD. (Psalms 25:7)

Often used as a substitute for "heaven's sake," or "for Christ's sake," the phrase "for goodness' sake" is a convenient euphemism for the less religiously oriented talker. David speaks in this passage of scripture and asks God to forget "the sins of my youth" in order to show "thy goodness' sake."

That is precisely why God does everything he does, for his "goodness' sake," not ours. Some might think this is selfish, but that accusation is wicked, for God created everything for his pleasure, not ours. He didn't create the universe because he needed someone to show his love to. That is heresy. God needs nothing, and that includes us. He is perfect and complete in all his ways, and out of his sheer mercy we are brought into a saving knowledge of him. To say that because God died for us so we must be infinitely valuable to him is a total perversion of the love of God. God died for "*his* goodness' sake," not ours, for we had none to die for anyway. Goodness sakes alive.

gospel according to...

> THE **GOSPEL ACCORDING TO** MATTHEW (Title of the book of Matthew)

Many will use this expression to belittle those that they think know it all or think they are right about everything. Three of the four gospels have this expression as their title, leading skeptics of the Bible to assert that these accounts can't be all God's words because they are just told "according to" each disciple.

Because there are differing facts in some accounts, this is somehow supposed to mean there are contradictions in the Bible. Any good lawyer knows that different witnesses of the same event will have extra or different information without it being necessarily contradictory.

Be careful Bible reader; God sets these traps to test your faith in his word. When in confusion, give his word the benefit of the doubt, and chalk up your misunderstanding to your ignorance, not his supposed mistakes.

greener pastures

> He maketh me to lie down in **green pastures**: he leadeth me beside the still waters. (Psalms 23:2)

People are always looking for something better or newer, whether it be a mate, a job, a car, etc. "If I could just get such and such, I'd be happy" is a lie because the Bible says, "The eyes of man are never satisfied." If you really want to find greener pastures, God, not the things of this world, will lead you to them.

guiding light

> And art confident that thou thyself art **a guide** of the blind, **a light** of them which are in darkness, (Romans 2:19)

Paul was reprimanding the Jews who felt they were "a guiding light" to convert the heathen—not knowing that they themselves needed converting. Feeling that you are a light to the blind when you yourself are blind is what Jesus meant in Matthew 6:23: "If therefore the light that is in thee be darkness, how great *is* that darkness!" As another biblical saying goes, "There is none so blind as those who will not see" (See John 9:39).

Religious deception is the worst kind, and it is the most effective tool of Satan who has "angels of light" that appear as "ministers of righteousness" (2 Corinthians 11:15). These ministers are in every denomination and religion on earth. That is what "Mystery Babylon" is referring to in Revelation.

H

half dead

> And Jesus answering said, A certain *man* went down from Jerusalem to Jericho, and fell among thieves, which stripped *him* of his raiment, and wounded him, and departed, leaving *him* **half dead**. (Luke 10:30)

The story of the Good Samaritan is familiar to most everyone. The man that the Samaritan helped had been robbed and hurt and was literally "half dead." Saying you're "half dead" means you're extremely exhausted.

This account serves as another of Jesus' rebukes to the religious leaders of his day, for this story involved a Levite priest that saw a wounded man but passed on by without helping. After the priest passed by, another man did help. The Bible does not say that this Samaritan was "good," just a neighbor. It is the unbeliever that wants to believe the Samaritan is "good," for it is the unbeliever that likes to assert that helping people makes you a "good" person.

God didn't teach us this story to show us how to get to heaven but to show us that even the unbelieving Samaritan helps those in need while some religious leaders ignore matters such as these.

half was not told me

> Howbeit I believed not the words, until I came, and mine eyes had seen *it*: and, behold, **the half was not told me**: thy wisdom and prosperity exceedeth the fame which I heard. (1 Kings 10:7)

"You haven't heard the half of it" is the expression we might use to describe a situation that has a lot of details yet to be revealed. This biblical context involved the Queen of Sheba's visit to King Solomon. According to Jesus, King

Solomon was the wisest man to ever live. Where Solomon got this wisdom, if you remember, was from his prayer to God at the dedication of the Jewish Temple that the king had built. When God asked him to name what he wanted, Solomon asked for wisdom.

Isn't it a sad commentary on man's nature that the wisest man to ever live, who also had everything he could ever want, summed up all his riches and wisdom as nothing but "vanity and vexation of spirit." "All is vanity," said King Solomon, and man's vanity is the very thing that refuses to let him acknowledge this.

hand in hand

> Though **hand *join* in hand**, the wicked shall not be unpunished: but the seed of the righteous shall be delivered. (Proverbs 11:21)

"Hand in hand" has come to be associated with lovers walking and holding hands or two people working closely together. The biblical usage refers to the wicked who unite "hand in hand" to accomplish some supposed great feat. Their unity does not impress God who says that in spite of their great deeds, they will not go unpunished.

The Bible seems to prophesy of very familiar happenings today. Events happen all the time where people join hands and literally form a human line that is miles long to raise awareness of different issues. Instead of placing your hands in union with the wicked, try, as the song says, to "Put your hand in the hand of the man who stilled the waters."

hardheaded

> As an adamant **harder** than flint have I made thy fore-**head**: fear them not, neither be dismayed at their looks, though they *be* a rebellious house. (Ezekiel 3:9)

Because Israel would not listen to God, God chose Ezekiel the prophet to speak unto them. He made the prophet's head "harder than flint" so that Ezekiel would not fear or "be dismayed at their looks." Being called "hardheaded" today means you have the reputation of not changing your mind despite other viewpoints. Being hard-headed for God means you don't compromise your position or belief in the face of adversity.

God likes hardheaded Christians, so don't let the world soften you up. While you're at it, go ahead and be narrow-minded also, for this pleases God as well (see "straight and narrow").

have nothing on someone

Hereafter I will not talk much with you: for the prince of this world cometh, and **hath nothing in me**. (John 14:30)

We've all heard criminal suspects who say, "You don't have anything on me" to a detective when the criminal does-n't believe he's guilty of some crime. Jesus uttered this statement about himself in reference to Satan whom he said "hath nothing in me."

Jesus was declaring he was perfect and without sin, so to say "Nobody's perfect" isn't quite true. The one who is "holy, harmless, undefiled, separate from sinners, and made higher than the heavens" is just that. In fact, all his children are considered spiritually perfect also: "For by one offering he hath perfected for ever them that are sanctified" (Hebrews 10:14).

There is a popular bumper sticker that says, "Christians aren't perfect, just forgiven." Someone's not reading his Bible.

he hung the moon (earth)

He stretcheth out the north over the empty place, *and* **hangeth the earth** upon nothing. (Job 26:7)

Who hasn't heard this expression? It is used to describe a person that another thinks very highly of, or, as we say, "worships the ground they walk on." One who believes that another "hung the moon" may not realize that that saying is "pushing the envelope" of blasphemy. God is the only one who hung the moon, and notice that the Bible actually said he did "hang" it. God never said anything about gravity holding all the planets and moons together, but he did say that he is "upholding all things by the word of his power" (Hebrews 1:3).

heart and soul

> Jesus said unto him, Thou shalt love the Lord thy God with all thy **heart, and** with all thy **soul**, and with all thy mind. (Matthew 22:37)

Giving all you can to accomplish something is the meaning of this biblical expression. According to Jesus and the Old Testament, loving God has to be done with heart and soul in order to obey the greatest commandment of all— "Thou shalt love the Lord thy God with all thy heart, and with all thy soul, and with all thy mind. This is the first and great commandment" (Matthew 22:37). It's all or nothing with God as far as your heart is concerned, so don't "lose heart" or go in "half-hearted," but "set your heart" on him, and he will give you your "heart's desire."

heart of stone

> And I will give them one heart, and I will put a new spirit within you; and I will take the **stony heart** out of their flesh, and will give them an heart of flesh. (Ezekiel 11:19)

"He has a good heart," people will say, or "His heart is in the right place," says some. Since God looks upon the heart and not the outside, his opinion is quite different from the norm. Everyone without God has a heart of stone and needs a new heart according to what God told Ezekiel: "I will take the stony heart out of their flesh, and will give them an heart of flesh."

hearts and minds

And the peace of God, which passeth all understanding, shall keep your **hearts and minds** through Christ Jesus. (Phillipians 4:7)

We speak of someone winning "the hearts and minds" of another group of people when a charismatic leader or influential person gets the affections and approval of his followers. For a Christian, the peace of God keeps "your hearts and minds through Christ Jesus." The peace of mind that everyone is looking for comes only from Jesus. Anything else is a false sense of security.

heart's desire

BRETHREN, my **heart's desire** and prayer to God for Israel is, that they might be saved. (Romans 10:1)

What we want most is what is meant by the phrase "heart's desire," and what Paul wanted most was for the Jews to be saved, of whom he said they were not.

That ought to go over well with the ecumenical movement today that teaches that all religions worship the same God. God will grant the ecumenical movement their heart's desire, the antichrist, a world leader that unites all the false religions. True Christianity just happens to be the only thing that keeps the antichrist from appearing, and when the Christians are taken up into heaven, there will be nothing to hinder his plans.

heaven on earth

¶ Therefore shall ye lay up these my words in your heart and in your soul, and bind them for a sign upon your hand, that they may be as frontlets between your eyes. And ye shall teach them your children, speaking of them when thou sittest in thine house, and when thou walkest by the way, when thou liest down, and when thou risest up. And thou shalt write them upon the door posts of thine house, and upon thy gates: That your days may be multiplied, and the days of your children, in the land which the LORD sware unto your fathers to give them, as the days of **heaven upon the earth**. (Deuteronomy 11:18-21)

History is full of man's futile attempts to create an earthly paradise. Utopian literature abounds, but the fact remains that man rejected heaven on earth in the Garden of Eden. The woman chose wisdom and to be like God by eating the fruit, and the man chose the woman by dying with her. Both, of course, were thrown out of this paradise for their disobedience.

If you deny that this literally happened, then you also deny the reason that Jesus paid for your sins, for Paul himself spoke of Adam and the redemption of mankind in Romans 5:19: "For as by one man's disobedience many were made sinners, so by the obedience of one shall many be made righteous."

heavy heart

As he that taketh away a garment in cold weather, *and as* vinegar upon nitre, so *is* he that singeth songs to **an heavy heart**. (Proverbs 25:20)

A heart that is weighed down with despair or trouble can be called a "heavy heart." In this passage from Proverbs, a heavy-hearted person should not have songs sung to him or music to cheer him up. This runs contrary to the prevailing opinion that music helps to soothe a sad person's emotions. The Bible says it makes matters worse and is likened to the reaction you'd get from taking a vagrant's garment from him in the winter. I guess we better think again about all these music ministries that minister to the depressed and downtrodden. They're making matters worse according to the Bible.

heat of the day

> Saying, These last have wrought *but* one hour, and thou hast made them equal unto us, which have borne the burden and **heat of the day**. (Matthew 20:12)

The hottest part of the day, i.e., "heat of the day," is not something most of us office workers experience with all of our air-conditioned comfort. We don't really have to make it by the sweat of our brow. The closest some of us get to sweating everyday is when we get in our car and it hasn't cooled off sufficiently yet.

The workers mentioned in this Bible passage were complaining that their co-workers got off easy by coming in at the "eleventh hour" (see phrase "eleventh hour"), and despite coming in late, they were paid the same wages. Those of us living in the eleventh hour of history will also get a much better deal than our ancestors, for some of us will escape death in the rapture.

here a little and there a little

> For precept **must be** upon precept, precept upon precept; line upon line, line upon line; **here a little, *and* there a little**: (Isaiah 28:10)

When a person speaks of the knowledge he has gained over the years, he usually refers to acquiring it "here a little, and there a little." This is how God desires we learn doctrine in the Bible, or else we will bite off more than we can chew.

Just like a baby must be weaned from his mother, we must first be weaned from the "milk of the word" before we can have the "strong meat" the Bible contains. Biblical breast-feeding is no different from the actual which God approves of as well (See Psalm 131:2). He doesn't expect us to keep drinking the milk of the word when there are big, juicy steaks in the book we haven't tasted yet.

here and there

And as thy servant was busy **here and there**, he was gone. And the king of Israel said unto him, So *shall* thy judgment *be*; thyself hast decided *it*. (1 Kings 20:40)

"Here and there" means various places, and its biblical usage hasn't changed. Many accuse the King James Bible of having archaic English, but as you can tell, the Bible seems to be popping up all the time in our conversation, archaic or not. Listen for these phrases in your conversations with others, and you will agree that the King James "archaic" phrases and words just don't seem to go away; instead, they are gaining in popularity.

"Here and there" has the equivalent "hither and thither" phrase also used in the Bible. "Hither and thither" and "*thee*'s and *thou*'s" may seem old-fashioned, but we use them more than we think. "With this ring, I thee wed" is used in plenty of marriages every year. School children sing, "My country 'tis of thee" every day. Shakespeare hasn't gone out of style because of his words like "*thinketh*," "*doth*," and his famous "Wherefore art thou?" The next time you want to update your Bible, maybe you ought to let it update you.

high-handed

And the LORD hardened the heart of Pharaoh king of Egypt, and he pursued after the children of Israel: and the children of Israel went out with an **high hand**. (Exodus 14:8)

To be high-handed is to be inconsiderate of others or not to consult others before doing something. The "high hand" that the children of Israel went out with refers to God's deliverance of them from Egypt. The modern and Biblical usages are somewhat connected. God acted high-handed and certainly didn't consult with anyone before delivering Israel. Anyone who does the same is considered presumptuous, and some ignorant souls will go so far as to say God is also. God does indeed act high-handed and has every right to do so, for he is the "Highest" (see Psalm 18:13). If you have any questions, please direct them to him.

high heaven

> *It is* as **high** as **heaven**; what canst thou do? deeper than hell; what canst thou know? (Job 11:8)

"That stinks up to high heaven," is a common use of this expression and means that something stinks so bad, it can be smelled all the way to heaven. What was "high as heaven" in the scriptures was God's wisdom according to Job's friend Zophar.

God's wisdom is not limited to the boundaries of heaven or hell. God is the only true "know-it-all" (see phrase) because he literally does know it all, and he doesn't mind it if you call him one—just mean what you say.

high noon

> And he said, Lo, *it is* yet **high day**, neither *is it* time that the cattle should be gathered together: water ye the sheep, and go *and* feed *them*. (Genesis 29:7)

"High noon" can mean exactly noon or refer to the apex or pinnacle of a person's endeavors. Although it is designated "high day" in Genesis, the sense is still the same. The phrase derives from the position of the sun in the sky which is highest at noon.

Despite our modern, digital, computerized timepieces, we still tell time as they did in biblical times—by looking where the sun is. "High noon" is another example of the freshness that the Bible adds to our language. It sure sounds more expressive than saying, "It's twelve o'clock."

his highness

> For destruction *from* God *was* a terror to me, and by reason of **his highness** I could not endure. (Job 31:23)

This expression is often used derogatorily for someone who acts "high and mighty," but who really isn't. Job used it literally and spoke of how he couldn't fight against God and "his highness," that is, his power and greatness. Job realized he was fighting a losing battle against the Lord, something most people don't ever figure out. However, this is how you "win by losing" as Jesus said: "...he that loseth his life for my sake shall find it."

hold my tongue

> For we are sold, I and my people, to be destroyed, to be slain, and to perish. But if we had been sold for bondmen and bondwomen, I had **held my tongue**, although the enemy could not countervail the king's damage. (Esther 7:4)

The prophet Habakkuk, along with countless others, wants to know why God "holds his tongue," or doesn't say anything, about the many evils that befall righteous people. The question, "If there's a God, why is there so much killing and suffering in the world?" is easily answered if you know your Bible. The answer is man's evil heart. Blaming God for the evil in the world is precisely what Adam did when God gave him a paradise to live in. Adam said the reason he ate the fruit was on account of the woman whom God gave him, thereby implicating God in his disobedience. "The Devil made me do it" is exactly what Eve said happened in the Garden of Eden.

Man blames anything but his own evil heart for his problems. The blame game is rampantly taking over this country's mentality. The problem with society lies not in anything other than our own heart, as Jesus himself said in Matthew 15:19: "For out of the heart proceed evil thoughts, murders, adulteries, fornications, thefts, false witness, blasphemies: These are the things which defile a man: but to eat with unwashen hands defileth not a man." Man has it all backwards as usual.

holier than thou

> Which say, Stand by thyself, come not near to me; for I am **holier than thou**. These *are* a smoke in my nose, a fire that burneth all the day. (Isaiah 65:5)

God accused the self-righteous Israelites of being holier-than-thou because they thought they were so much better than others that they didn't want others coming near them. God also said this attitude was a "smoke in my nose."

Today, the secular crowd calls any religious person "holier-than-thou" that they deem a threat to their lifestyle of sin. The religious person might respond that he is not holier-than-thou, but just trying to live for God. What both sides don't realize is the fact that the believer *is* holier than the unbeliever. God said believers are "holy brethren" (Hebrews 3:1), "an holy priesthood" (1 Peter 2:5), and "an holy people unto the LORD" (Deut. 7:6). This doesn't mean that, as a believer, you sin less than unbelievers, but rather, you have been justified and made holy by God himself. Go ahead and tell the world you are holier than they are and watch "the sparks fly" (see expression "watch the sparks fly").

Holy Land

> And the Lord shall inherit Judah his portion in **the holy land**, and shall choose Jerusalem again. (Zechariah 2:3)

Why does the whole world continue to fight over an extremely small piece of land in the Middle East? The Jews, Christians, and Muslims all realize the significance of Israel, especially Jerusalem. It is indeed holy to all three, but in the end, Jesus himself shall own it and rule from his throne in Jerusalem when he returns.

If God came down and walked in your land, you'd probably not want to give it up either. Isn't it strange that the news media doesn't call any other lands on earth "the Holy Land" but the true one itself, Israel?

Holy of Holies

> And after the second veil, the tabernacle which is called **the Holiest of all**; (Hebrews 9:3)

"Curiosity killed the cat," they say. It also would literally kill anyone who dared venture into "the holiest of all," the place where God's glory appeared in the Jewish Tabernacle. Only the high priest could go in, and only once a year could he do that. If he did not follow God's instructions to the letter (see phrase "to the letter"), God would kill him on the spot.

The world has taken this phrase and applied it to any secret chamber, special place of reverence, or off-limits area within a building. A person seeking God today doesn't need to travel to some far away monastery or temple to find him. This is why God actually ripped the veil separating the holiest of all from the rest of the Tabernacle, for he wanted "the holiest of all" (himself) to be accessible to all. The "Authorized Personnel Only" sign no longer applies, and thank God for it.

holy water

> And the priest shall take **holy water** in an earthen vessel; and of the dust that is in the floor of the tabernacle the priest shall take, and put *it* into the water: (Numbers 5:17)

Some churches like to throw their holy water on everything and make it better, and others like to take their holy water and sprinkle it on people's heads to make them holy. God did say the Jews had "holy water" to use for special occasions, but today's use of holy water is another instance of trying to assimilate Jewish law in to Christianity, something not meant to be. Nobody in scripture got saved by having water poured on his head, and Satan never trembled at anyone who threw water at him in some exorcism.

These kinds of exorcisms and baptisms and their use of holy water amount to nothing more than religious magic spells, a practice God likens to witchcraft. If water helps to save you, then water is your savior.

hope against hope

> Who **against hope believed in hope**, that he might become the father of many nations; according to that which was spoken, So shall thy seed be. (Romans 4:18)

To "hope against hope" is to believe, like Abraham, that something hoped for will come to pass when there is almost no chance it will. Abraham believed that his wife would have a child at 100 years of age and that this child's descendants would eventually produce the Messiah, Jesus Christ.

"Hoping against hope" is comparable to saying, "You don't have a prayer," but that's exactly what they both had. God answered Abraham's prayer, and Sarah had a child. This miraculous birth foreshadowed another one, namely, that of Jesus Christ. Although Mary didn't have to change diapers at 100 years of age like Sarah, Noah had them all beat, for his wife had a child when Noah was 500 years old.

Having trouble believing that people lived this long and had babies at these ages? Maybe you're going to have to exercise a little faith and try believing the scriptures as they're written; otherwise, you're forced in "hoping against hope" that the Bible's wrong, and that is a spiritually hopeless situation. The prudent thing would be to err on the cautious side and go ahead and believe it. God will explain it to you later.

house divided

> And Jesus knew their thoughts, and said unto them, Every kingdom divided against itself is brought to desolation; and every city or **house divided** against itself shall not stand: (Matthew 12:25)

Known for its usage in Lincoln's famous Civil War speech, the expression "house divided" comes from the passage in Matthew in which Jesus' old adversaries, the Pharisees, were accusing him of being in league with the Devil. Because Jesus was casting out devils, he was accused of getting help from Beelzebub, the prince of the devils. Thus, when God was on earth, he was accused of worshipping the Devil!

What greater contradiction against God could there be? This is what is meant in Hebrews 12:3 where it said that Jesus "endured such contradiction of sinners against himself." Our light afflictions pale in comparison.

how are the mighty fallen!

The beauty of Israel is slain upon thy high places: **how are the mighty fallen**! (2 Samuel 1:19)

In this day and age of sports heroes and entertainment icons, we are always seeing some of the famous lose all integrity because of scandal or behavior; hence, the phrase "how are the mighty fallen" is used to describe their fall. Whether it be religious superstars, entertainment icons, or sports heroes, God repeatedly knocks them down off their pedestal. He does this to show their followers that God is a jealous God who will not tolerate these icons receiving all this adoration which amounts to nothing more than idolatry.

Americans like to think they are not idolaters like some cultures that worship trees and rocks, but America has its own "trees and rocks," and more of them at that than any other nation, even with all of America's supposed knowledge and sophistication.

I

if need be

Wherein ye greatly rejoice, though now for a season, **if need be**, ye are in heaviness through manifold temptations: (1 Peter 1:6)

Peter spoke of the saints' faith being tried "if need be" through many temptations. Though God doesn't tempt any man according to James chapter one, he does "try him every moment" as stated in Job 7:18. When the world says these are "trying times," the Christian knows this better than anyone.

in all his glory

And yet I say unto you, That even Solomon **in all his glory** was not arrayed like one of these. (Matthew 6:29)

To be "in all your glory" signifies that you are showing off peculiar attributes, good or bad, that truly exemplify yourself to others. It can also mean you are stark naked! When the multitudes were worried about things like food and clothing, Jesus told them to "Consider the lilies of the field, how they grow; they toil not, neither do they spin: And yet I say unto you, That even Solomon in all his glory was not arrayed like one of these." Jesus said a flower was grander than the richest king's splendor. He sure knew how to put things in perspective, wouldn't you say?

Speaking of glory, the saints will literally be "in all their glory" when they "appear with him in glory" (Col. 3:4), and when they receive "the obtaining of the glory of our Lord Jesus Christ" (2 Thess. 2:14). Thus, a Christian is the only one who can literally be said to be "in all his glory."

in God we trust

> **In God** have **I** put my **trust**: I will not be afraid what man can do unto me. (Psalms 56:11)

What person is on every coin and paper bill in America? Well, it's not "Old George" or "Honest Abe," but God himself, except he didn't get his picture on them, just his name. No matter how hard the atheists try, they just can't get the U.S. to remove the saying "In God We Trust."

"Trust me," is the cry we hear from so many these days. A Christian's response to the question, "Don't you trust me?" should be "No, I don't, and I shouldn't according to scripture."

We are, of course, not to put our trust in man, as the context of the phrase "In God we trust" indicates. As a Christian, we are not even supposed to put our trust in other Christians. God certainly doesn't, as stated in Job 15:15: "Behold, he putteth no trust in his saints: yea, the heavens are not clean in his sight." God can't count on any man, but man can definitely count on God.

in God's hands

> FOR all this I considered in my heart even to declare all this, that the righteous, and the wise, and their works, *are* in **the hand of God**: no man knoweth either love or hatred *by* all *that is* before them. (Ecclesiastes 9:1)

Watching the 1994 NBA Finals between the Houston Rockets and the New York Knicks, you might have noticed the expression "In God's hands" written, of all places, on the head of one of New York's players. He obviously thought the outcome of the game depended on God's will, thus the phrase "in God's hands." Based on that, God must be a Houston Rockets fan, for the Rockets won the world championship.

in the heat of battle

> And he wrote in the letter, saying, Set ye Uriah **in the** forefront of **the hottest battle**, and retire ye from him, that he may be smitten, and die. (2 Samuel 11:15)

Sporting events, particularly football and hockey, often give rise to confrontations that are the result of the intense competition or the "heat of the battle." David meant this expression literally in the Bible when he ordered Uriah to go to the front lines of battle. He did this hoping to get Uriah killed so he could have Uriah's wife Bathsheba for himself. Bathsheba was the one who David saw bathing in the infamous "shower scene" in scriptures.

Some skeptics like to point to this shower scene and other passages in scripture that get sexually descriptive and call it pornography, thus accusing God of writing smut. The Song of Solomon, a whole book dedicated to the sexual pleasures of two lovers, is a prime example used by these accusers. The book compares the woman's breasts to "clusters of grapes" and in another place says, "Thy two breasts are like two young roes that are twins." Just because the world doesn't know the difference between love and lust doesn't mean God doesn't either.

in the spirit

> I was **in the Spirit** on the Lord's day, and heard behind me a great voice, as of a trumpet, (Revelation 1:10)

To do something "in the spirit" of someone or something means that one is agreeable and enthusiastic about something or is in harmony with it. The apostle John was literally "in the spirit" when he was caught up to heaven and shown visions of God and the future. The phrase has become so watered down today that it has nothing to do with God.

It is not always advisable to act in the spirit of something because you may be participating in another spirit—the spirit of antichrist mentioned in I John 4:3. The

Bible says there is "another Jesus," "another spirit," and "another gospel" in 2nd Corinthians chapter eleven. The book of John says "God is a Spirit," but not "God is Spirit" as some versions like to put it, implying that all spirit is God.

The world likes to talk about the spirit of famous dead people being with us in some fashion, not knowing that God says, "the spirit shall return unto God who gave it" (Ecclesiastes 12:7). Maybe some other kind of spirit is hanging around these people.

in your right mind

And they come to Jesus and see him that was possessed with the devil, and had the legion, sitting, and clothed, and **in his right mind**: and they were afraid. (Mark 5:15)

When God performs an exorcism, he doesn't need two priests battling for hours to get the job done as is commonly portrayed in movies. Jesus, and even Paul, cured demon-possessed people instantly and completely, so completely, in fact, that afterwards, one was said to be "in his right mind," or completely normal. This wasn't just any so-called demon possession, for this man that Jesus cured had broken chains that were put on him and was seen mutilating himself and hanging around tombs.

Bring one of these actual demon-possessed people to a "religious revival" and watch the "healers" scatter.

it is high time

And that, knowing the time, that now *it is* **high time** to awake out of sleep: for now *is* our salvation nearer than we believed. (Romans 13:11)

"It's about time," we might say, or "The time is now," or "There's no time like the present." The coming of Jesus approaches quickly, and the church, according to Paul here in Romans, needs to wake up and smell the coffee. The world, of course, doesn't believe it's high time to awaken out of their sleep; instead, they believe the night is young. The Bible declares, "the night is far spent, the day is at hand" (Romans 13:12).

The Bible talks also about the world being in a drunken-like state of deep sleep concerning the Second Coming: "...they are drunken, but not with wine; they stagger, but not with strong drink. For the LORD hath poured out upon you the spirit of deep sleep, and hath closed your eyes: the prophets and your rulers, the seers hath he covered" (Isaiah 29:10).

When God makes you drunk, it's not with wine, but it's a lot more powerful. If God makes you drunk, you're not going to sober up until you let God wake you up with his word.

J

jot and tittle

> For verily I say unto you, Till heaven and earth pass, one **jot or one tittle** shall in no wise pass from the law, till all be fulfilled. (Matthew 5:18)

If you work with contracts or detailed paperwork, you can appreciate this phrase. It is an equivalent to "dotting your "*i*'s" and crossing your "*t*'s," i.e., paying attention to details. If you want to know God's attitude towards his book, this quotation by Jesus should provide you with that. His book contains jots, tittles, letters, and words. To alter any of these is tantamount to changing the whole book.

To show the importance of a single letter, the apostle Paul based a whole doctrine on the letter "*s*," the difference between "*seed*" and "*seeds.*" In Galatians 3:16, he makes his case: "Now to Abraham and his seed were the promises made. He saith <u>not</u>, And to <u>seeds</u>, as of many; <u>but</u> as of one, And to thy <u>seed</u>, which is Christ."

The next time you're in a biblical discussion and someone says you're arguing "semantics," tell this person that semantics is exactly what you should be debating. Ask any lawyer how much semantics matter, and he'll tell you that it is not only the words that matter, but also the letters themselves. And by the way, don't think commas and capital letters can't change the whole meaning of a text—they can.

Judgment Day

> Verily I say unto you, It shall be more tolerable for the land of Sodom and Gomorrha in **the day of judgment**, than for that city. (Matthew 10:15)

All unbelievers will "get their day in court," unfortunately, for them, the judge will be Jesus Christ, and the true

Judgment Day will begin. The defendant will be his own lawyer, and there will be no trial by jury. There will be no adjudicated probation or shortened sentences for good time. The death penalty is not an option, for it would be a relief; instead, they get the proverbial "fate worse than death" and fulfill that saying literally.

If found guilty of rejecting Jesus as God and Savior, the unbeliever will be thrown into a lake of fire to be tormented day and night forever. There will be no appeals and no witnesses called. The possibility of a complete pardon does exist, but it must be obtained from Jesus himself before the trial begins. No law degree is needed for that.

jump for joy

Rejoice ye in that day, and **leap for joy**: for, behold, your reward *is* great in heaven: for in the like manner did their fathers unto the prophets. (Luke 6:23)

We usually use "jump for joy" sarcastically to show we really don't like something. For example, if one tells you something he thinks will excite you, and you're not particularly thrilled, you might say it makes you "jump for joy" to be facetious.

Jesus told us to actually "jump," and he said to do it for a reason we wouldn't expect. In verse twenty-two of the above reference, he had this to say: "Blessed are ye, when men shall hate you, and when they shall separate you *from their company*, and shall reproach *you*, and cast out your name as evil, for the Son of man's sake. Rejoice ye in that day, and leap for joy."

When's the last time you leaped for joy when someone said he hated your guts? You probably wanted to leap for his throat, not in the air. A true Christian realizes he will be hated and expects to be so. Jesus said if people hated him, whom they did, they will hate us also.

K

keep the faith

> I have fought a good fight, I have finished *my* course, I have **kept the faith**: (2 Timothy 4:7)

Not wavering, waffling, or turning back on what you're believing or doing would qualify you as "keeping the faith." Even the secular crowd has a similar saying: "If you don't stand for something, you'll fall for anything." Paul said he didn't compromise his beliefs and was ready to receive his crown in heaven. Notice it said that there is "the faith," which teaches that there is only one.

Compromise in matters of faith and other areas of our life is praised today as a noble quality to possess. For a Christian to compromise would be the "kiss of death" (see "kiss of death").

Compromise supposedly shows evidence of our tolerance, but God never told us to compromise or tolerate anything. Everything may not be so black and white all the time, but it will be right or wrong, for right and wrong does not come in different shades.

kill the fatted calf

> And he said unto him, Thy brother is come; and thy father hath **killed the fatted calf**, because he hath received him safe and sound. (Luke 15:27)

Another way of saying, "Let's have a dinner party" is to tell everyone you're going to "kill the fatted calf." This expression originates from the famous Prodigal Son story told by Jesus. After his wayward son returned home, the father welcomed him with open arms, an obvious parallel to God and the sinner.

"Killing the fatted calf" may not appeal to you vegetarians out there, but celebrating with vegetables only wasn't this father's idea of a party. Before you slaughter your next "fatted calf," make sure the animal rights activists don't see you, or you'll get an ear full. Kill all the unborn babies you want though. (Maybe they ought to think twice about killing babies; aren't they supposed to be evolved from animals too?) The hypocrisy in this matter is rather deafening, don't you think?

kingdom come

> Thy **kingdom come**. Thy will be done in earth, as *it is* in heaven. (Matthew 6:10)

The more popular meaning of "kingdom come" is to die; it also means something will take so long a time in coming that it probably won't occur. An example of each would be something like the following: "We would all be blown to kingdom come if a nuclear bomb was dropped on our country," or "You can keep arguing till kingdom come, but I won't change my mind."

Taken from the Lord's Prayer, "kingdom come" alludes to the kingdom of Jesus coming to earth at his return. At his coming, Jesus really will blow millions to kingdom come because he will literally kill millions before and during the battle of Armageddon. The Bible describes this horrifying event in Isaiah 63:2-3: "Wherefore *art thou* red in thine apparel, and thy garments like him that treadeth in the winefat? I have trodden the winepress alone; and of the people *there was* none with me: for I will tread them in mine anger, and trample them in my fury; and their blood shall be sprinkled upon my garments, and I will stain all my raiment. For the day of vengeance *is* in mine heart, and the year of my redeemed is come."

This might explain how "kingdom come" has come to mean dying. Yes, God kills, and he will kill more people than anyone in history. For a detailed account of this mass killing, see the book of Revelation, chapter six and nine, where God talks about killing <u>most of the world</u> through judgments of all sorts. "I kill, and I make alive; I wound, and I heal" (Deuteronomy 32:39).

know-it-all

Hast thou perceived the breadth of the earth? declare if thou **knowest it all**. (Job 38:18)

The only real know-it-all (because he does literally know everything) is Jesus Christ. Anyone else that is called that name acts as if he has all knowledge, something akin to what Job did when God asked him some rather tough questions, questions he couldn't answer if he had tried.

God was showing the finiteness of Job in comparison to the Lord himself. God does indeed have all the answers, but unless you have the right questions, his answers won't do you any good.

L

labor of love

Remembering without ceasing your work of faith, and **labour of love**, and patience of hope in our Lord Jesus Christ, in the sight of God and our Father; (1 Thessalonians 1:3)

A hobby or job that one does for the sheer pleasure that he gets from it can be called a "labor of love." Paul commended the church at Thessalonica for their work for the Lord. For any true Christian, doing the Lord's work is an honor and is naturally a labor of love. For those who don't like doing the work of God such as witnessing, teaching, and helping others, but you do it anyway, your labor is in vain.

land of giants

And the rest of Gilead, and all Bashan, *being* the kingdom of Og, gave I unto the half tribe of Manasseh; all the region of Argob, with all Bashan, which was called the **land of giants**. (Deuteronomy 3:13)

Remember the old television show called "Land of the Giants" where the little people were always hiding from the giants? The Bible mentions giants, so naturally this word is ridiculed and scoffed at by skeptics as being false. What the Bible referred to as "giants" were men that were nine to ten feet tall, sometimes taller.

There is archaeological evidence for these men, and we've even had modern examples of men that grew to almost nine feet tall (see the *Guinness Book of World Records*). The Israelites mentioned seeing giants in the land of Canaan and said they were the sons of Anak. Of course, we all know the story of Goliath, the giant of Gath, and how David killed him with a slingshot.

If you own a one of the newer versions other than a King James, you better not use it to teach that David killed Goliath because that fact is contradicted. These versions teach someone else killed Goliath in 2 Samuel 21:19-20. That omission is a giant one indeed.

land of milk and honey

And I am come down to deliver them out of the hand of the Egyptians, and to bring them up out of that land unto a good land and a large, unto a **land flowing with milk and honey**; unto the place of the Canaanites, and the Hittites, and the Amorites, and the Perizzites, and the Hivites, and the Jebusites. (Exodus 3:8)

Sounds like an enormous candy bar or some recipe for a sore throat, but this expression was a description of the fertile lands of Israel. By extension, a "land of milk and honey" has come to mean any fertile land ripe for settlement.

God promised the land of the Canaanites to the Hebrew slaves; hence, God took someone else's land and gave it to the Hebrews. This is the root of the controversy in the Middle East today. If you want to blame God for all the fighting in the Middle East, go ahead. Remember, though, that the land really belongs to God anyway, and he can do whatever he wants with it (see "promised land"). Since he started this conflict, he also will end it at his return.

land of the living

But where shall wisdom be found? and where *is* the place of understanding? Man knoweth not the price thereof; neither is it found in **the land of the living**. (Job 28:12-13)

The "real world" is a saying with the same meaning as the colorful expression "land of the living." It is often used to welcome back people who have stayed out of the public eye for some reason. This meaning hasn't changed much from the biblical usage where Job mentioned that wisdom wasn't found in the "land of the living."

The apostle Paul adds to this teaching when he said, "the wisdom of this world is foolishness with God." Try posting that on some college billboard. Real wisdom comes from the scriptures, not your college professor who teaches in the "land of the living."

law unto themselves

> For when the Gentiles, which have not the law, do by nature the things contained in the law, these, having not the law, are **a law unto themselves**: (Romans 2:14)

Disobeying established authority and setting yourself up as your own judge makes you "a law unto yourself." As with many of these expressions, the Bible's use of it is literal, not figurative. Paul spoke of the Gentiles' own conscience serving as the law that would judge them because of their lack of a written law at that time.

God, then, agrees with the adage "Let your conscience be your guide," because God's laws are "written in their hearts" (verse 15). Only to the extent that you don't have a Bible and can't get one will your conscience be your guide. In this day and age, you can get a Bible just about anywhere for little or no cost. Man will be without excuse at Judgment Day because God has put right and wrong in his heart.

There is a point, however, that the wicked reach when even their conscience can't guide them anymore because it has become "seared with a hot iron" according to 1 Timothy 4:2. Since one may never quite know when he reaches that stage, it's very dangerous to delay getting saved. You might want to put a "rush" on that order.

lay at the door of...

> If thou doest well, shalt thou not be accepted? and if thou doest not well, sin **lieth at the door**. And unto

thee *shall be* his desire, and thou shalt rule over him. (Genesis 4:7)

Anything said to be "lying at the door" usually signifies that something bad is getting ready to happen to that person. God stated that sin was lying at the door of Cain if he didn't do well. He also said that sin would "rule" over Cain, and that "sin" would be Cain's desire.

Sadly, this is the case for every sinner, for sin rules over everyone who has not defeated it through Christ. Paul stated in Romans 6:6-7 that sin doesn't rule over the Christian: "Knowing this, that our old man is crucified with *him*, that the body of sin might be destroyed, that henceforth we should not serve sin. For he that is dead is freed from sin." In Romans 6:14, he teaches that "...sin shall not have dominion over you: for ye are not under the law, but under grace."

If sin is lying at your door, you can bet it will get its foot in, so don't "play around with fire" as the saying goes (see "play with fire"). Sin is the biggest and most powerful "Pandora's box."

lay down your own neck

Who have for my life **laid down their own necks**: unto whom not only I give thanks, but also all the churches of the Gentiles. (Romans 16:4)

To sacrifice yourself for another is the present as well as the biblical meaning for "lay down your own neck." The apostle Paul expressed his affection for his friends Aquila and Priscilla whom he said "laid down their own necks" for him. The measure of true love, according to Jesus, is found in John 15:13: "Greater love hath no man than this, that a man lay down his life for his friends."

The fact that God actually laid down his own neck on the cross provided us with the single greatest act of love ever shown. God did not send someone else to die for us; he himself became a Son by being born. That's why Jesus is called the "only begotten Son" in John 3:16. In that passage, it stated that God gave his "only begotten Son," or in other words, his only born son. In 1 John 3:16, the Bible states very clearly who actually died for us: "Hereby perceive we the love *of God*, because he laid down his life for us: and we ought to lay down *our* lives for the brethren." What greater sacrifice and act of love could God have shown us?

lay it to heart

> If ye will not hear, and if ye will not **lay *it* to heart**, to give glory unto my name, saith the LORD of hosts, I will even send a curse upon you, and I will curse your blessings: yea, I have cursed them already, because ye do not **lay *it* to heart**. (Malachi 2:2)

"Laying a matter to heart" means seriously considering something and its relevance to you. The Bible mentions that when the righteous die, no one seems to care, implying that the unrighteous receive all the attention and concern. Of course, the wicked need all the pomp they can get at a funeral. The righteous know their destiny is heaven, but isn't it strange that every deceased person at a funeral is said to go to heaven? No one ever seems to go to hell at these occasions. Everybody must become a Christian at death, or so it seems.

If we are not to judge a person's salvation (even though we are because "he that is spiritual judgeth all things"), then why does everyone judge that the deceased is in heaven? It is hypocrisy, and for anyone to participate in falsely comforting someone about their loved one's decease by saying he's in heaven now when the deceased may not be a believer makes a liar out of him, not a caring sympathizer.

left hand doesn't know what the right hand is doing

> But when thou doest alms, let not thy **left hand know what thy right hand doeth**: (Matthew 6:3)

Jesus taught that if you give alms, i.e., charity, it should be done in secret. Apparently, this command for anonymous giving doesn't stop those who give huge donations and have whole buildings named after them. Even the Christian should refrain from his name being plastered on walls of church buildings or having his name associated with gifts given. Christians shouldn't need a pat on the back—they'll get their rewards later.

The phrase "left hand doesn't know what the right hand is doing" as used today speaks of a group of people working together but pulling in different directions because they're unorganized or are being given conflicting orders; in other words, they're not all on the same page. How's that for defining an expression with another expression! One sure way people can truly and literally be on the same page is for them to get their marching orders from the Bible.

The only way you can be on the same page from the Bible is for all to be in the same Bible, or you will have confusion. Go to any church today, and you will see the congregation all reading out of various versions of the Bible that are <u>vastly different</u> from each other. Not only does the left hand not know what the right hand is doing, neither are many members literally on the same page. The preacher reads a passage out of a newer version, and half his congregation can't effectively listen to him because they're each in a version of their choice.

Try to imagine a classroom teacher teaching a group of students with each student reading from a different, re-translated textbook. The effect of the teaching would be no different than the effect of the preaching—it would be chaos and confusion. The student could always say his answers are based on his book, so there would be no single, correct answer.

This is what is happening to the church today. Naturally, this alienates us from God, "For God is not *the author* of confusion, but of peace, as in all churches of the saints."

let come what may

> Hold your peace, let me alone, that I may speak, and **let come on me what *will*.** (Job 13:13)

"Let the chips fall where they may," "Whatever happens, happens,"—these are similar in meaning to the biblical expression that Job used when he told his detractors that no matter what happened to him, he would say to God, "...let come on me what will." Job's faith and trust in God is legendary and is exemplified in his statement two verses later: "Though he slay me, yet will I trust in him: but I will maintain mine own ways before him."

The world might have to rely on chips falling where they may or supposed good luck, but the Christian shouldn't believe in or rely on luck. The scriptures don't wish us "good luck," but say in Romans 8:28: "And we know that all things work together for good to them that love God, to them who are the called according to *his* purpose." For a Christian to tell somebody "good luck" is to agree with the world that God is not in control of our affairs. Lady Luck and Father God are not soul mates.

let nature take its course

> And the tongue *is* a fire, a world of iniquity: so is the tongue among our members, that it defileth the whole body, and setteth on fire the **course of nature**; and it is set on fire of hell. (James 3:6)

The Bible says in the next two verses that man has tamed every type of animal, yet man's tongue remains untamed and can't be tamed, for "it is an unruly evil, full of deadly poison." To "let nature take its course" implies that nature operates in a systematic way, or by course, and that it will take care of itself as long as man's tongue doesn't set it on fire.

Nature doesn't have a mind of its own, but only operates and takes its course because of what God has programmed it to do. How else would animals have the instincts they do if it weren't for those instincts having been put into the animals in the first place?

God tells man that despite man's taming of animals, he can't tame himself. Man needs his own animal trainer, and that trainer can be none other than Jesus Christ. He's been known to crack a few whips before. See the book of Matthew.

like father, like son (like mother, like daughter)

¶ Behold, every one that useth proverbs shall use *this* proverb against thee, saying, **As *is* the mother, *so is* her daughter**. (Ezekiel 16:44)

Any parent can attest to this adage because he knows his children will, in part, reflect his own values. Children are the fruit of their parents, and a "tree is known by its fruit" according to Jesus. The same idea holds true in the spiritual sense as well. Jesus told the Pharisees in John chapter eight: "Ye are of *your* father the devil, and the lusts of your father ye will do." Jesus was teaching that the wicked would behave like Satan because the wicked are children of their spiritual father the Devil. Other scriptures like 1 John 3:10 and Acts 13:10 confirm this teaching. For example, the apostle Paul has no problem telling it like it is when he says in Acts 13:10: "O full of all subtilty and all mischief, thou child of the devil, thou enemy of all righteousness, wilt thou not cease to pervert the right ways of the Lord?"

You are either a child of God or a child of the Devil according to the Bible; there is no in-between state or neutrality with God, for Jesus himself said that you are either for him or against him. The prevailing notion that all people are God's children is obvious heresy based on the above references. The typical people who haven't been saved are just as much children of the Devil as the overt Satan worshippers that wear black robes and sacrifice animals and so forth; the Satanists just have the guts to admit who they are while most others don't. The Bible makes no distinction between the overt Satan worshipper and other wicked men; man does so to make himself feel better.

like putty in my hand

> O house of Israel, cannot I do with you as this potter? saith the Lord. Behold, **as the clay _is_ in the potter's hand**, so _are_ ye in mine hand, O house of Israel. (Jeremiah 18:6)

Being called "putty in my hand" is considered a derogatory comment because the person that is labeled "putty" is thought to be easily manipulated by others. The Christian, however, considers it an honor to be putty in God's hands, for the clay, or putty, does not tell the potter how to shape it according to Romans 9:20: "Nay but, O man, who art thou that repliest against God? Shall the thing formed say to him that formed _it_, Why hast thou made me thus?"

The picture of the spinning clay pottery being formed on the potter's wheel is the analogy that God wants us to imagine because he is rounding all our rough edges and shaping us into a beautiful vessel. God even calls us "vessels" in 1 Thessalonians 4:4. Vessels are used to pour liquid into, and God pours his spirit into each vessel he creates. We could all use a few lessons in the potter's class.

little bird told me

> ¶ Curse not the king, no not in thy thought; and curse not the rich in thy bedchamber: for **a bird of the air shall carry the voice**, and that which hath wings shall tell the matter. (Ecclesiastes 10:20)

Surprisingly, this expression finds its origin from the book of Ecclesiastes. We use it today when we want to hide from someone how we came to know a particular matter. In the context of this phrase, the Bible warns us not to curse others because it might be told by a "bird of the air."

The fact that God used birds in this expression is not without significance, for birds are sometimes representatives of devils (see Matt.13:32 and Rev. 18:2). Thus, the Bible hints that devils can inform others of your secrets, so think before you curse others, or it can literally come back and haunt you.

little by little

> **By little and little** I will drive them out from before thee, until thou be increased, and inherit the land. (Exodus 23:30)

God told Israel he would drive out their enemies "by little and little." This idea has application in the spiritual sense in that God drives out our enemies, or sin, little by little so that we can learn the power of sin and the power of God to defeat it.

God, if he wanted, could give all of us lives without sin or death to deal with. But we should thank God for sin and death, for without it, many of us would not need, depend on, or seek God. Death, though tragic, is also a tool that God uses to bring us closer to him.

Because we are to thank God in everything ("In every thing give thanks"), we should not hesitate to thank him for sin and death instead of always questioning why someone has to suffer or die.

live by the sword, die by the sword

> Then said Jesus unto him, Put up again thy sword into his place: for all **they that take the sword shall perish with the sword**. (Matthew 26:52)

A very appropriate philosophy of modern-day street gangs, this saying originated from the mouth of Jesus at the time of his arrest and betrayal by Judas. Peter pulled out his sword and cut off the ear of one of the high priest's servants when they tried to arrest Jesus. Jesus rebuked him for cutting off it off and actually put it back on without plastic surgery. Notice, however, that Jesus didn't rebuke Peter for having a sword, only for misusing it. In fact, in another place, he told his disciples to take up the sword.

By extension, then, owning a weapon, including a gun, is a Christian's right and obligation and is not in conflict with biblical teaching; to the contrary, it is a tenet of it. Peter carried his weapon wherever he went, and Jesus never told him to get rid of it.

live for one's self

> And *that* he died for all, that they which live should not henceforth **live unto themselves**, but unto him which died for them, and rose again. (2 Corinthians 5:15)

Everybody lives for something, whether it be money, fame, work, family, etc. If there comes a time when these don't matter anymore, we say we have "nothing to live for," but that is precisely the time when one should realize that it is Jesus whom we really should be living for.

The whole Christian walk is the process of not living for one's self but living for the one who died for them. Telling someone to "get a life" is what the Christian has actually done, for he got "the way, the truth, and the life."

live off the fat of the land

> And take your father and your households, and come unto me: and I will give you the good of the land of Egypt, and ye shall eat **the fat of the land**. (Genesis 45:18)

To "live off the fat of the land" is to live in luxury or to enjoy the best a place has to offer. Pharaoh told the Israelite Joseph, his second-in-commmand, that he and his family had that privilege in his country.

The "name it, claim it; blab it, grab it; believe it, receive it" crowd in Christendom teaches that it is the Christians' lot in life to have it all. Paul taught otherwise and said that we should be content to have food and clothing (1 Timothy 6:8). Omitted was the need for a nice home, satellite dishes, computers, cars, college, retirement pensions, insurance, or any other modern "necessities."

We in America have been living off "the fat of the land" for years, but it's just a matter of time before all of this luxurious living comes to a screeching halt. America faces a judgment of God that will be swift, sure, and devastating.

lord and master

Ye call me Master and Lord; and ye say well; for *so* I am. If I then, *your* **Lord and Master**, have washed your feet; ye also ought to wash one another's feet. (John 13:13)

This expression is often a sarcastic euphemism for one's husband and if used in the literal sense would be scoffed at today. As a man, if you tell society that you are your wife's lord and master, they will probably have a good laugh. Despite society's ridicule of this title, God does call the husband the wife's "lord": "Even as Sara obeyed Abraham, calling him lord:" "Loving and obeying" in the wedding vows is quickly disappearing today.

If the wife would recognize that the man is the "master of the house," she wouldn't have any problem obeying him. Men are called "the master of the house" (Judges 19:23) several times in scripture, but never the woman. We obey our bosses because they have the final authority at our jobs, so why do some have problems with God placing that final authority with the husband? You can't have two masters at home or the job. Both would be a trainwreck waiting to happen.

Lord have mercy

Have mercy upon us, O **LORD, have mercy** upon us: for we are exceedingly filled with contempt. (Psalms 123:3)

Commonly used as an exclamation of help or astonishment, this biblical expression is meant literally by

King David who wanted God's mercy granted unto him continually. Pleading for mercy occurs often in courtrooms, and because of mitigating factors, it is sometimes given by the judge. God, the judge of all, always grants mercy to those who sincerely ask for it.

"Lord have mercy" has been so overused that many of us may not realize it is a plea for God to shed his mercy on us because of our sins, for sinners need all of God's mercy they can get. If you don't have it, don't leave this earth without it, or "Lord have mercy!"

lost and found

> For this my son was dead, and is alive again; he was **lost, and is found**. And they began to be merry. (Luke 15:24)

We normally look for valuables in the "lost and found" of some establishment if we can't find them, but on the bigger scale, God looks in the heavenly "lost and found," for to him the whole human race could be classified as "lost and found" in his eyes because they're either saved (found) or lost (damned).

"Lost and found" occurs in the story of the Prodigal Son which referred to the wayward son who "was lost, and is found." "Lost" is the right description for the sinner who doesn't have spiritual direction in his life. Just like the lost traveler, the sinner rarely admits that he is lost. What we really need is a bunch of lost and found signs with the words "Lost-Mankind, Reward-Salvation" on them. If you'll notice, there's always an abundance of items (and humans) lost, but few are found.

M

make a name for yourself

> And they said, Go to, let us build us a city and a tower, whose top *may reach* unto heaven; and let us **make us a name**, lest we be scattered abroad upon the face of the whole earth. (Genesis 11:4)

Trying to get recognition and prestige for yourself defines this expression from the book of Genesis. The builders of the ill-fated Tower of Babel tried to "make a name for themselves," and God showed them how he felt about this by destroying the tower and making all mankind speak different languages.

The existence of languages like Chinese, Russian, German and others with all their vast differences and complete lack of connection to each other only goes to show that this judgment at Babel really could have and did happen. The world's languages could not have come about as the result of some linguistic evolution. There are dialects everywhere of major languages, but to say that English could have gradually descended from Chinese, or Swahili is related to Russian is beyond belief.

Those who study this issue are forced by logic not to believe in linguistic evolution and forced to believe in this account of the Tower of Babel, but of course, that's not going to help them to "make a name for themselves" in the secular or even Christian world. If you choose not to make a name for yourself, then you'll end up "making a spectacle of yourself" as evidenced in the next paragraph.

make a spectacle of yourself

> For I think that God hath set forth us the apostles last, as it were appointed to death: for **we are made a**

spectacle unto the world, and to angels, and to men. (1 Corinthians 4:9)

Drawing attention to yourself in a foolish way is considered "making a spectacle of yourself." Paul said that the apostles are "made a spectacle unto the world" and, in like manner, so are all Christians. A believer is accounted as a "fool for Christ's sake" because of his witness, actions, and beliefs.

People will ridicule you for believing in talking snakes (the garden of Eden), Noah's ark, 900-year-old men (Genesis 5), people making the sun stand still (Joshua), and so on. If you dread making a spectacle of yourself because of your fear of man, go ahead and avoid, deny, or explain away these occurrences, and you'll fit right in with every other unbeliever who fears "making a spectacle of himself." The Bible, like Travis in the Alamo, definitely draws a line in the sand for us to decide."

make light of

But they **made light of** *it*, and went their ways, one to his farm, another to his merchandise: (Matthew 22:5)

In the parable of the marriage of the king's son, the invited guests made light of their invitations and went their own ways in much the same way that some make light of being invited to the marriage supper of the lamb, Jesus Christ.

"Making light," or joking, is forbidden by scripture. This might come as a shock to even Christians who like to tell jokes. Ephesians 5:3-4 puts joking (jesting) in the same category of offenses as fornication: "But fornication, and all uncleanness, or covetousness, let it not be once named among you, as becometh saints; neither filthiness, nor foolish talking, nor jesting, which are not convenient: but rather giving of thanks." "There is a time to laugh," says God, but this is not equivalent to joking. Good, "clean jokes" were never told by Jesus, the apostles, or any Christian in scripture.

God characterized the false prophets in the Old Testament by their constant practice of making light of matters. Why then do so-called Christian preachers feel the need to be comedians in the pulpit? The real jokes are those who try to be Christians and comedians.

make short work of

For he will finish the work, and cut *it* short in righteousness: because **a short work** will the Lord **make** upon the earth. (Romans 9:28)

"To make short work of" a task means to complete it in a hurry. The work that God is finishing in the above verse is the saving of a remnant of Israel in the last days. Israel did not become a country again in 1948 for the first time in 1,900 years for no reason. God is getting ready to use Israel in his plans for the Great Tribulation that precedes the Second Coming. He has not forgotten about his chosen people and will save some of them at this time. What God started with the patriarch Abraham 4,000 years ago he will finish in the coming years. If anyone can "make a short work" of something, it is the Lord.

make your hair stand on end

Then a spirit passed before my face; **the hair of my flesh stood up**: (Job 4:15)

Job's friend Eliphaz reminded Job in this passage that suffering came because of sin. Eliphaz recounted how a "spirit" (he didn't say it was God) appeared and spoke to him, giving Eliphaz wisdom (how many times do we hear that today!). Job was not impressed with his friend's wisdom or visions, as we should not be when others come up and pull the same stuff on us. Eliphaz said, "...the hair of my flesh stood up"; i.e., he was terrified.

God's spirit shouldn't terrify *believers*, so what Eliphaz saw was probably a manifestation of a devil. The Christian world today has many people seeing so-called "visions" and supposedly hearing many voices. If you want to hear God's voice, then read his words, for they are his voice according to the book itself. You won't have to wonder whose voice you're hearing.

man after your own heart

> But now thy kingdom shall not continue: the LORD hath sought him **a man after his own heart**, and the LORD hath commanded him *to be* captain over his people, because thou hast not kept *that* which the LORD commanded thee. (1 Samuel 13:14)

A person "after your own heart" shares your beliefs and values, akin to a soul mate. When King Saul reigned over Israel, the prophet Samuel told the king that because of Saul's disobedience, God sought "a man after his own heart" to be the next king of Israel. That man turned out to be David. In like manner, anyone who has "kept that which the Lord commanded" can also be a man after God's own heart.

man child

> And when the dragon saw that he was cast unto the earth, he persecuted the woman which brought forth the **man child**. (Revelation 12:13)

An immature adult or extremely large baby could be called a "man child." The Bible's use of "man child" is quite the opposite, for it designates Jesus Christ as the "man child" in the book of Revelation, but of course, Jesus was never overweight or immature.

Jesus must have acted like a man even when he was a little child because he confounded the scholars in the temple at the age of twelve with his biblical wisdom. It is always amusing but sad to see Christian children today who confound unlearned adults with their wisdom.

man of the house

And wheresoever he shall go in, say ye to **the goodman of the house**, The Master saith, Where is the guestchamber, where I shall eat the passover with my disciples? (Mark 14:14)

Because of today's divorce rate, this expression, which refers to the father of a family, is becoming less and less applicable. In too many homes today, there is no man of the house, and in a lot of those homes where the man is there, he certainly doesn't act like one.

Jesus spoke of a certain house where he wanted his disciples to eat the Passover supper and called the owner the "goodman of the house." Jesus implied that this man was the head of the house just as the Bible does in other passages where it calls the man the "master of the house." The Bible specifically calls the husband "the head of the wife" in Ephesians 5:23, and in Genesis 3:16, God told Eve that her "desire *shall be* to thy husband, and he shall rule over thee."

You can almost hear the feminists screaming right now, can't you? These women like to accuse the Bible of teaching anti-feminist doctrine, and it does, for it says there are certain duties of a wife and certain ones for a husband. Equality has nothing to do with it, but that is usually the excuse given for opposition to this teaching.

man of the world

Arise, O Lord, disappoint him, cast him down: deliver my soul from the wicked, *which is* thy sword: From men *which are* thy hand, O Lord, from **men of the world**, *which have* their portion in *this* life, and whose belly thou fillest with thy hid *treasure*: they are full of children, and leave the rest of their *substance* to their babes. (Psalms 17:14)

Though used to describe cultured, sophisticated men, "men of the world" is what David asked God to deliver him from. A Christian should never consider it a compliment to be called a "man of the world." How you feel about worldly people and things is a surefire test of how you feel about God. "If any man love the world, the love of the Father is not in him."

Only you know if you love God or not. The evidences of your salvation include this list from 2 Corinthians 7:11: "For behold this selfsame thing, that ye sorrowed after a godly sort, what carefulness it wrought in you, yea, *what* clearing of yourselves, yea, *what* indignation, yea, *what* fear, yea, *what* vehement desire, yea, *what* zeal, yea, *what* revenge! In all *things* ye have approved yourselves to be clear in this matter."

Wondering if you're a man of God instead of a man of the world? This list would be a good measuring stick to evaluate your salvation and how it affected you. Notice that the characteristics of being saved include fear, indignation and revenge, qualities you don't hear too much about from all the milk toast, cotton candy Christianity being espoused today.

manna from heaven

And had rained down **manna** upon them to eat, and had given them of the corn **of heaven**. (Psalms 78:24)

What we all would like during our time of need is some manna from heaven, an unexpected, timely, even miraculous gift like the Israelites got in the desert when they had no food to eat. Actual "manna from heaven," a type of bread, came down from the skies to feed the Israelites during their exodus through the desert.

Little do people realize that this miraculous food from the sky wasn't a one-time event. God continued this feeding every day for *forty years* as stated in Exodus 16:35. The Israelites complained, however, because they longed for some other food, saying in Numbers 11:5-6: "We remember the fish, which we did eat in Egypt freely; the cucumbers, and the melons, and the leeks, and the onions, and the garlick: But now our soul *is* dried away: *there* is nothing at all, beside this manna, *before* our eyes."

The Israelites were saying they had it better in Egypt, and this highly displeased the Lord. God decided to give them quail to eat, but because of Israel's longing to go back to Egypt, he was going to give them so much quail that it was going to "come out at your nostrils" (see other expression) according to Numbers 11:20.

This story had a tragic ending, if you remember, because the Lord killed all the Israelites who complained even "while the flesh was yet between their teeth." This account gives new meaning to this common dinner prayer: "Let us be grateful for what we are about to receive."

many a time

Many a time have they afflicted me from my youth: yet they have not prevailed against me.   (Psalms 129:2)

A quaint way of saying you have experienced something rather frequently is by using the expression "many a time." This saying finds its origin from the book of Psalms where King David speaks of the afflictions he received from the wicked occurring "many a time."

Life is no bed of roses for a Christian, for "Many *are* the afflictions of the righteous: but the LORD delivereth him out of them all."

meat and drink to someone

For the kingdom of God is not **meat and drink**; but righteousness, and peace, and joy in the Holy Ghost. (Romans 14:17)

Anything important, essential, or pleasurable to you could also be designated as your "meat and drink." Exercise is meat and drink to any athlete as book reading is to a scholar. The modern usage of this phrase differs from its biblical counterpart. In Romans, Paul teaches that "meat and drink" are not concerns of those in the kingdom of heaven.

What a concern food is, however, for those on earth! Think of the time we spend buying, preparing, eating, and cooking food, and don't forget about the dishes! Eating consumes a substantial part of the average person's life.

Will we eat food in heaven? Jesus ate broiled fish and honeycomb after he ascended to heaven and came back down to earth, and angels ate food given to them in the Old Testament, so it can be concluded that Christians after death can do the same. We won't need this food to keep us alive, since we will be perfected in body and soul.

Pizza, ice cream, and fried chicken will probably not be on the menu. Our diets will most likely consist of what Adam and Eve had in the garden, but we won't have to worry about any forbidden fruit. We will be eating from the bread of life of whom it is said, "he that cometh to me shall never hunger; and he that believeth on me shall never thirst."

meet your maker

> Therefore thus will I do unto thee, O Israel: *and* because I will do this unto thee, prepare to **meet thy God**, O Israel. (Amos 4:12)

We will all "meet our maker" one day, for we will be face-to-face with the creator of the universe, Jesus Christ. God told a backsliding Israel that because of their sins, he was getting ready to kill them and told them they should "prepare to meet thy God."

At issue with believers today is whether or not you meet your maker immediately after death or at the return of Jesus Christ for his saints (the rapture). There is a substantial amount of biblical evidence for the doctrine of soul sleep which states that the soul actually sleeps with the body until its resurrection at the rapture. Christians that are passed away are described as "sleeping" throughout scripture, including Lazarus whom Jesus raised. The Bible talks about the spirit going back to God who gave it, but not the soul.

Given that this doctrine is true, it would overthrow the mainstream teaching that everyone at death goes to heaven or hell right away. We've all heard preachers try to comfort the loved ones of a deceased person by saying, "They're with Jesus right now." This, then, would not be true. Souls don't go to heaven without being first judged, and the Bible does not talk about 10 billion separate Judgment Days, one for each person in history. There is one judgment of believers and the "Great White Throne" judgment of the unbelievers mentioned in the book of Revelation. A judge does not sentence a criminal without first sentencing him at his trial. No sinner is going to hell at his death, or heaven for that matter, without first having God the judge of all sentence him also.

millstone (albatross) around your neck

But whoso shall offend one of these little ones which believe in me, it were better for him that a **millstone were hanged about his neck**, and *that* he were drowned in the depth of the sea. (Matthew 18:6)

A heavy burden of responsibility one has to bear is also called an "albatross around the neck" or "millstone" as the scripture calls it. The context of this phrase has Jesus speaking of children who believed in him and what a grave offence it was if others corrupted these children and their beliefs. Jesus said these evil corrupters would be better off if they had "drowned in the depths of the sea" because the punishment that awaits them is much worse than they can imagine.

Jesus was not saying all children are innocent, for there comes a time when they must exercise faith and believe in him. Exactly when that time is varies with each child, but it is near the time when they can understand the gospel of how they are a sinner and how Jesus paid for their sins with his death.

There's coming a day (it's already here in part) when the gospel is going to be considered mental abuse because you're supposedly hurting the child's self-esteem by telling him he is wicked and needs saving. Refusing to tell a child that he is in danger of hell fire is the real child abuse, and that is something that qualifies you to have your own "millstone around the neck."

mind your own business

> And that ye study to be quiet, and to **do your own business**, and to work with your own hands, as we commanded you; (1 Thessalonians 4:11)

"Keeping your nose out of other people's affairs" is the meaning of this biblical expression from Paul's letter to the Thessalonians. Scripture admonishes the believer in another passage not to be "busy bodies," but, instead, "with quietness they work, and eat their own bread."

Working is a commandment of God, and those who refuse aren't supposed to get charity or even food given to them. "For even when we were with you, this we commanded you, that if any man would not work, neither should he eat" (2 Thessalonians 3:10). Giving all these "homeless" people food to eat who stand all day on street corners begging for money when they are perfectly capable of working is not loving them; it is an act of sin and rebellion against the word of God. We should rebuke the homeless person (beggar) who refuses to work and then we would be showing them compassion. Your should either believe the Bible and refuse to support someone who will not work, or you will perpetuate his condition by supporting his slothfulness.

morning, noon, and night

Evening, and morning, and at noon, will I pray, and cry aloud: and he shall hear my voice. (Psalms 55:17)

"Morning, noon, and night," as used in this scripture, is not an prescription for the exact times you should pray as the Muslims have adopted, but it is an admonition to pray at all times as it states in 2 Thessalonians 3:17: "Pray without ceasing." This expression is used to emphasize something that happens constantly; thus, it retains the biblical meaning as well. Notice that the Bible says evening comes first, for the biblical day starts with the night and ends with the day-light. Naturally, this parallels the way the true light, Jesus, conquers the night (evil).

Saying that our day starts with the morning and ends with the night does away with the parallel that God intended for us to make. God has a reason for everything he writes, and this is why in Genesis 1:5 he said, "And the evening and the morning were the first day." A Jewish day still begins at 6:00 P.M., but western civilization (no surprise) reverses this biblical teaching.

mother of all...

And Adam called his wife's name Eve; because she was **the mother of all** living. (Genesis 3:20)

The Persian Gulf War made this expression popular again when Saddam Hussein said that it would be "the mother of all battles" meaning the greatest and grandest of all. The Bible used this phrase in the literal sense again, referring to Eve as the actual "mother of all living."

If you like tracing your family tree, you might not know all of it, but you will know who your oldest relatives are because we all came from the same parents, Adam and Eve. The "mother of all" of us was Eve. The question often comes up as to how Adam and Eve could have accounted for all the different races in the world. The answer could easily be that God made Eve's three sons a different ethnicity, for Adam had all the genes of future man in his body.

This is another trap for the unbeliever who looks for excuses not to believe the scriptures. Does it never occur to him that there may be answers he hasn't considered? What an evolutionist has to believe is that the astronomically impossible process of evolution not only occurred once at the start, but, in fact, had to have happened several times in different places on the globe by chance to account for the different races he sees today. He is forced to believe in multiple occurrences of evolution taking place in multiple places at once, or believing in God's account that says very simply that Eve was the "mother of all living." Believing in this evolutionary theory has to rank as "the mother of all" fairy tales.

N

next of kin

¶ None of you shall approach to any that is **near of kin** to him, to uncover *their* nakedness: I *am* the LORD. (Leviticus 18:6)

Frequently, we hear this expression used when someone dies or is killed. The name of the deceased won't be released until the next of kin is notified, i.e., his closest relatives. "Kin" is a country dialect, and the Bible contains other examples of country talk. David says "many a time" in Psalm 78:38; Peter said in John 21:3 that he will "go a fishing"; Jesus told his disciples in Matthew 26:36 to "Sit ye here, while I go and pray yonder." Our word "britches" (breeches) is used in Exodus 28:42; King David talked about "a mess of meat" in 2 Samuel 11:8, and David asked whether God's mercy was "clean gone" forever in Psalm 77:8.

The Bible is truly a book for all people, appealing to the scholar, the common man, and the unlearned through its use of differing styles of language. It's even a little bit "country."

night is young (far spent)

The night is far spent, the day is at hand: let us therefore cast off the works of darkness, and let us put on the armour of light. (Romans 13:12)

One beer company's commercial encourages you to drink up, for it says the "night is young." This company's ad is a twist on the original rendition from the Bible which stated the complete opposite idea: "The night is far spent." When you hear someone say, "The night is young," say to him that the Bible says it's not. The Bible stresses that it's time to wake up because the "night" (evil works) has now been conquered by the "morning star," Jesus Christ.

no rest for the wicked

> There is **no peace**, saith my God, **to the wicked**. (Isaiah 57:21)

People never seem to have enough time to do the things they need to do on a daily basis anymore. One characteristic of the wicked is their refusal to rest and observe times of peace and quiet (see "peace and quiet"). "Workaholics" have to keep busy in order to feel good about themselves, but the righteous enjoy rest for physical and spiritual reasons.

God instituted the day of rest (the seventh day) not only for spiritual time but also to rest our bodies to rejuvenate us for the following week. Literally speaking, there really is "no rest for the wicked" if they are working seven days a week. America's five-day workweek, however, allows too much rest and doesn't obey one of the Ten Commandments of God: "Remember the sabbath day, to keep it holy. Six days shalt thou labour, and do all thy work" (Exodus 20:8-9). We are commanded to work six days, not five. God instituted the seventh day for us to observe each week to remind us of the coming rest we will have in the thousand-year reign of Jesus.

Since Hebrews chapter four and Revelation chapter twenty speak of the seventh day as a period of rest that Christians will experience at the return of Christ, and since this period is a thousand years, Bible readers have concluded that the other six days could each stand for a thousand years as well. Thus, they say, the six days of creation also was prophetic in that God was giving man in Genesis a timetable of future events. The earth would last 6,000 years to the return of Christ, and the seventh day would then begin with the thousand-year reign of Christ. According to Bible chronology, we are nearing 6,000 years since the world was created, which means Christ's return could be closer than you think. Depending on whom you are, that could cause some more restless nights.

nothing new under the sun

> The thing that hath been, it *is that* which shall be; and that which is done *is* that which shall be done: and *there is* **no new *thing* under the sun**. (Ecclesiastes 1:9)

Go into any supermarket and you'll always see products advertising something "new," "advanced," or "improved." Science and technology continually bombard us with the newest research and inventions. According to God, none of this is new whatsoever. We are always discovering things about ancient civilizations that show they had advanced ideas in science or math that we previously thought only we had.

Even in the Bible, there are numerous scientific facts that were supposedly only "discovered" in this modern era but have been in the Bible for thousands of years. For example, the idea that all the continents were joined together at one time and eventually split apart was stated in Genesis 10:25 rather succinctly over 4,000 years ago: "And unto Eber were born two sons: the name of one *was* Peleg; for in his days was the earth divided; and his brother's name *was* Joktan." The fact that the earth is a sphere and not flat as was believed in the Middle Ages could easily have been discredited with a reading of Isaiah 40:22: "It is he that sitteth on the circle of the earth." Another proof that the earth was a sphere was the words of Jesus in Luke 17:30 and 34. Jesus says that when he returns it will be day and night at the same time. He says it would be day in verse thirty and night in verse thirty-four. That could only happen if the earth was a sphere, which was supposedly not known at that time. Bacterial germs were known about in Leviticus 15:13, for it was required for a person to "bathe his flesh in running water, and shall be clean." This is why the Jews didn't get sick during the Black Plague when germs were responsible for that outbreak that killed millions. The Gulf Stream that helps England in the winter with its warm waters goes through the middle of the Atlantic. God talked about "springs of the sea" in Job 38:16. Even automobiles were prophesied in Nahum 2:3-4: "...the chariots *shall be* with flaming torches in the day of his preparation, and the fir trees shall be terribly shaken." In the next verse, it even foretold freeways, traffic, and accidents: "The chariots shall rage in the streets, they shall justle one against another in the broad ways: they shall seem like torches, they shall run like the lightnings." There are many more of these scientific facts and prophecies, including nuclear war and space travel. The Bible has always been way ahead of its time and is much more scientific than it usually gets credit for. There's really "nothing new" about that though.

now hear this

> Therefore **now hear this**, *thou that art* given to pleasures, that dwellest carelessly, that sayest in thine heart, I *am*, and none else beside me; I shall not sit *as* a widow, neither shall I know the loss of children: (Isaiah 47:8)

Commonly used as an attention-getting gimmick over a megaphone or microphone, this adage was employed by God to warn Babylon of its coming judgments. It was a serious warning then, but now it is usually relegated to a practical joke, as when someone is trying to act as if an important announcement is going to be made, and they say, "Now hear this, now hear this."

God won't need any public address system to announce his coming to the earth. "For the Lord himself shall descend from heaven with a shout," it says in 1 Thessalonians 4:16. Instead of the "*shot* heard 'round the world," God will have his "*shout* heard round the world."

O

oh my God!

> **O my God**, my soul is cast down within me: therefore will I remember thee from the land of Jordan, and of the Hermonites, from the hill Mizar. (Psalms 42:6)

A plea for help and a cry to God has been turned into a trite saying that is used so much that it has lost its original force and is now used just the same as an ordinary exclamation like "Wow" or "Gee." Even heathen, atheists, and agnostics occasionally exclaim "Oh my God" despite the fact they don't really believe in him.

Isn't it ironic that God gets them to call on him and quote his Bible even when they profess to hate him? There is no escaping the influence of the Bible on lives of the ordinary citizen because God will make sure you learn of him whether you want to or not.

oh spare me!

> **O spare me**, that I may recover strength, before I go hence, and be no more. (Psalms 39:13)

"Spare me, please" is the cry of those who don't want to hear something or who disapprove of a matter rather strongly. David asked God to literally spare him, or preserve his life; thus, the meaning has changed again from literal to figurative though there is a slight connection still to the biblical usage.

If you ask someone to spare you of something distasteful or unfavorable, you are pleading with him to not hear his talk. You want him to spare you because what he's saying is "killing you"; thus, you're asking him, symbolically, to spare your life as David did to God.

old days

> The Lord hath done *that* which he had devised; he hath fulfilled his word that he had commanded in **the days of old**: he hath thrown down, and hath not pitied: and he hath caused *thine* enemy to rejoice over thee, he hath set up the horn of thine adversaries. (Lamentations 2:17)

The old days always bring back fond memories for those of us who can remember the way things used to be. With things changing so fast these days, there are fewer and fewer things to remind us of the way life was many years ago.

The Bible is certainly a living link with the old days, some parts of it having been around for 3,500 years. God's word is the one item that most all our families over scores of generations have shared. The fact that our lives are being shaped today by the same book that our ancestors had thousands of years ago is astounding, and it is a testament to the enduring value of this amazing book. The old days will always be here in part as long as we have the Bible.

old wives' tales

> But refuse profane and **old wives' fables**, and exercise thyself *rather* unto godliness. (1 Timothy 4:7)

"Old wives' tales" is a term used for various superstitions and folk tales that have been passed down over the years. The expression probably refers to the times when most wives stayed home and supposedly had more idle time to gossip and spread false notions among themselves.

Though society today expects women to work outside the home, the Bible commands a woman to be a "keeper at home" (Is this where we get the term housekeeper?). In 1 Timothy 5:14, the apostle Paul says, "I will therefore that the younger women marry, bear children, guide the house, give none occasion to the adversary to speak reproachfully." Of course, there are exceptions for widows and single mothers.

A phrase like "old wives' tales" and society's attitude in general shed a negative light on the stay-home mom, but the greatest responsibility a woman has is raising children and instructing them at home. A big reason for the destruction of the American family is that other people and things are raising our children, be it the public schools, day-care centers, baby-sitters, the television, etc. The greatest child abuse today is the neglect of our children by the parents themselves. It's very difficult to "honour thy father and thy mother" when the child is hardly with them.

once and for all

By the which will we are sanctified through the offering of the body of Jesus Christ **once _for all_**. (Hebrews 10:10)

So many religions today, including mainline denominations, teach that you get to heaven by believing and earning your way there. Unless you go to church, give money, ask for forgiveness, be baptized, do good deeds, speak in tongues, etc., they say you will not make it to heaven or will be in danger of losing your salvation. They will tell you that Jesus is "the way," but they will also tell you indirectly that they are "the way to the way."

Religious bondage takes on many forms, but to teach that Jesus saves you by himself without the help of the church altar or baptismal font, and that Jesus will forever keep you saved without the need of church service every Sunday and Wednesday just doesn't pay dividends to the many churches who practice this religious slavery.

How about letting the Bible settle this issue? We are sanctified (saved) "through the offering of the body of Jesus Christ once _for all_." If the blood of God didn't pay for all of your sins, (past, present, and future), then nothing did. Anything added to that sacrifice would make a mockery of the greatest act of love ever shown to mankind.

one and the same

> But all these worketh that **one and the selfsame** Spirit, dividing to every man severally as he will. (1 Corinthians 12:11)

Writing about the spiritual gifts to the church, Paul was making the point that though there were diversities of operations and administrations of God; it was all done by the "same spirit" (verse four), the "same Lord" (verse five), and the "same God" (verse six).

It is this writer's contention that the Father, Son, and Holy Ghost are not only the same God, but they are one and the same spirit. Claiming that Jesus is the same God as the Father and the Holy Ghost but denying that they are the same spirit would negate the fact that they are the same God. If the Father, Son, and Holy Ghost are not one and the same spirit, then God is three distinct spirits. They are the same Lord, Spirit, and God according to verses four through six. That is the meaning of "one and the selfsame spirit."

Since man was created in God's image and likeness, all of us bear a resemblance to him. Therefore, we all have one soul, one body, and one spirit just as God does in the person of Jesus Christ. Jesus and God are "one and the same."

one way or another

> Go thee **one way or other**, *either* on the right hand, *or* on the left, whithsoever thy face *is* set. (Ezekiel 21:16)

God told Ezekiel the prophet to either go "one way or other," to the right or to the left, and God would cease his judgments on Israel. The expression "one way or another" refers to the desire to get something done no matter what it takes.

If we analyzed this phrase more closely, we would recognize that it conveys some biblical truth. There is only "one way" or "another"—Jesus' or Satan's. There is the "broad way" or the "narrow way" according to Matthew chapter seven. Going with the flow (the broad way) will have you ending up in the sewer. Going against the flow will get you splattered with a lot of the world's muck. It's time to roll up our sleeves.

out of sight, out of mind

> I am forgotten as a dead man **out of mind**: I am like a broken vessel. (Psalms 31:12)

"How soon we forget" goes the old saying. When someone you have shared company with no longer sees you, or when you ignore a matter for a time, you tend to forget about it because it is "out of sight, out of mind." David was lamenting over the fact that no one seemed to be mindful of his plight, so he said he felt like a "dead man out of mind."

Fortunately, for those who keep the Lord out of sight, out of mind, he doesn't do the same, for if he did, none of us would get saved. "The LORD hath been mindful of us: he will bless *us*" (Psalm 115:12). We will never be out of sight and out of mind with him, and that is, as they said in the Sixties, "out of sight man."

out-of-the-body experience

> I knew a man in Christ above fourteen years ago, (whether in the body, I cannot tell; or whether **out of the body**, I cannot tell: God knoweth;) such an one caught up to the third heaven. (2 Corinthians 12:2)

Paul recounted how he knew a man who was "caught up to the third heaven" and heard things he said were "not lawful for a man to utter." Some believe Paul was referring to himself in the third person, speaking of the time he was stoned and left for dead.

Regardless of who is being talked about, we hear this type of thing occurring regularly. For example, people are always claiming to have died clinically, gone to heaven, saw lights, and felt total peace, etc. Did you ever notice that none of these people ever seem to die and get a vision of hell?—it's always heaven. Out-of-the-body experiences, however, are nothing new, and you can bet we will all participate in one at the time of our death—some just get a little preview, like Paul.

out of the mouth of babes

> **Out of the mouth of babes** and sucklings hast thou ordained strength because of thine enemies, that thou mightest still the enemy and the avenger. (Psalms 8:2)

Little children have a way of stating the simple truths that we as adults often overlook. The simple, yet blunt truth, will often come from a child and can teach us many things. On the other hand, to use this expression to teach that little children always speak the truth is wrong. Children are natural born liars, and for that matter, so are *babies* according to Psalm 58:3: "The wicked are estranged from the womb: they go astray <u>as soon as they be born, speaking lies</u>." How do infants speak lies, you ask? Become a parent and you'll find out. Little babies are capable of deceiving us without us even realizing it. They learn to cry for things even when they're not upset, and this is not learned but bred in them.

P

parting of the ways

> For the king of Babylon stood at the **parting of the way**, at the head of the two ways, to use divination: he made *his* arrows bright, he consulted with images, he looked in the liver. (Ezekiel 21:21)

After not reaching an agreement on a matter because it can't be resolved, people might have what is called "a parting of the ways." The apostle Paul, to much surprise, had one of these "parting of the ways" arguments with one of his disciples. Barnabus wanted to take John along with Paul to visit several churches Paul had established. Paul was adamant about not taking John as it states in Acts 15:38-9: "But Paul thought not good to take with them, who departed from them from Pamphylia, and went not with them to the work. And the contention was so sharp between them, that they departed asunder one from the other."

In the context of Ezekiel where "parting of the ways" occurs, the king of Babylon, after coming to a fork in the road, was confused about which way to go, so he tried just about anything to help him including witchcraft and looking in livers. How a liver can tell you which direction to take has to qualify as one of the stranger ways to get your bearings, but, then again, when you don't have God to lead you, you might try anything.

pass the time

> And if ye call on the Father, who without respect of persons judgeth according to every man's work, **pass the time** of your sojourning *here* in fear: (1 Peter 1:17)

When there's nothing to do and you're looking for something to help occupy your time, God says to "pass your time" in fear. In Proverbs 23:17, the Bible says to "Let not thine heart envy sinners: but *be thou* in the fear of the LORD all the day long."

Instead of killing time, the Christian's obligation is "Redeeming the time, because the days are evil." A Christian's response to the question "What's goin' on?" should never be "Nothin' much," but rather something like this: "I'm passing my time in the fear of the Lord." That'll get a big "Huh?"

passed away

> *One* generation **passeth away**, and *another* generation cometh: but the earth abideth for ever. (Ecclesiastes 1:4)

To say a friend or loved one has died can be a little harsh for some, so saying this person "passed away" softens the blow a little even though this phrase may not be as spiritually accurate as discussed earlier on soul sleep. Jesus did say a soul passes from death unto life at his rebirth in John 5:24. The question of whether there is life after death is answered throughout scripture.

In reality, we all have life after death whether we want it or not. The issue is not whether there is life after death, but will there be *death after life* for those who don't believe in Jesus. The book of Revelation calls the torment in hell "the second death"; thus, Christians have a saying related to this: "If you're born twice, you die once. If you're born once, you die twice." The choice is a second birth or a second death. Birth is always a much more pleasant experience.

patience of Job

> Behold, we count them happy which endure. Ye have heard of **the patience of Job**, and have seen the end of the Lord; that the Lord is very pitiful, and of tender mercy. (James 5:1)

James, the brother of Jesus (Mary wasn't always a virgin), instructed his brethren to be patient concerning the coming of the Lord, for many saints were growing restless for his return. To understand the expression "patience of Job," you would have to have read the account of Job and his sufferings to appreciate his patience on God.

As it turned out, Job lost everything—his family, his health, his fortune, and his friends. Throughout his ordeal, and despite occasional weakness, Job believed in the goodness of God. In the end, God gave him back double of what he lost.

Though the patience of Job is quite commendable, the patience of God is exceedingly more so. God waits our entire lives sometimes just to change us even if it requires the deathbed conversion.

patience of a saint

> Here is **the patience of the saints**: here *are* they that keep the commandments of God, and the faith of Jesus. (Revelation 14:12)

Along the same lines as "the patience of Job," this expression is probably more popular and refers to the time of the Great Tribulation and the reign of the Antichrist. During this tumultuous time, the saints are exercising their patience in waiting on Jesus by refusing to take the mark of the beast, and most will give their lives in order to avoid taking this mark.

It needs to be pointed out that common Christians are called "saints," not just the "important" ones, as is the practice in some churches (see Jude 14; Phillipians 1:1; Deut. 33:2, etc.). Any believer is just as much a saint as any of the well-known ones such as St. Christopher, St. Joseph, or any others.

No one ever prays to these saints in the scriptures or wears them around his neck for good luck. Paul never instructed anyone to pray to him or Peter or anybody. That is idolatry no matter how you justify it, and that means it's an abomination in the sight of God. Praying to anybody or anything other than Jesus Christ is the worship of a false god regardless of reasons for it.

peace and quiet

> And the work of righteousness shall be **peace; and** the effect of righteousness **quietness** and assurance for ever. (Isaiah 32:17)

The cry of every parent with obnoxious children is for a little "peace and quiet." Those who need peace and quiet can have exactly that if they get saved, for the Bible says that the righteousness you get from God will bring about "peace; and the effect of righteousness quietness." Consequently, a wicked person can never truly have peace and quiet even if he surrounds himself with life's pleasures, for "There is no peace, saith my God, to the wicked."

pearl of great price

> ¶ Again, the kingdom of heaven is like unto a merchant man, seeking goodly pearls: Who, when he had found one **pearl of great price**, went and sold all that he had, and bought it. (Matthew 13:45-6)

Whatever you hold dear or highly treasure could be called your "pearl of great price." Some teach that Jesus is the pearl of great price and that this passage refers to man selling everything he has and buying Jesus. The opposite is the case. The real pearl of great price is man himself, whom Jesus Christ bought with the highest price of all—his life. 1 Corinthians 6:20 say "ye are bought with a price." Christ purchased us; we did not purchase him and can't. Acts 20:28 said that ministers should "feed the church of God, which he hath purchased with his own blood."

God's use of the pearl to describe the people he saved is very instructive. The process by which a clam makes a pearl parallels the process by which God makes a Christian. A pearl starts out as a small fragment of a rock or dirt that acts as an irritant to the clam. The clam covers the wretched particle with the beautiful covering of pearl, layer by layer. We are the dirt, and God is the clam. The only way, though, that the dirt gets changed is to get inside the clam.

The pearl has other qualities that make it unique among jewels. It is the only precious jewel that is the product of a living thing, just as we are the product of a living God. The fragment transforms into a pearl, rising from the muck of the ocean floor to become a precious jewel. Pearls also can't be cut or divided as other jewels can, and no two pearls are exactly alike.

Job knew of these things when he wrote: "But ask now the beasts, and they shall teach thee; and the fowls of the air, and they shall tell thee: Or speak to the earth, and it shall teach thee: and the fishes of the sea shall declare unto thee." Some of the best teachers are not people, but things. We can all enroll in that course.

pearly gates

And the twelve **gates *were* twelve pearls**; every several gate was of one pearl: and the street of the city *was* pure gold, as it were transparent glass. (Revelation 21:21)

The commonly quoted misconception that Peter stands at "the pearly gates" checking our names on the list is not biblically accurate. Actually, there are twelve angels standing at twelve different gates of pearl, not Peter. Many people don't realize that these pearly gates are part of the superstructure of the gigantic city called "New Jerusalem." This city is described as being in the shape of a cube, fifteen hundred miles ("fifteen thousand furlongs") long, wide, and high. The whole city is surrounded by a wall that is 144 cubits high (over 300 feet).

Since this city will be on earth at the time of the Millennium, there will be unbelievers on the outside who will not be allowed in. Membership requirements are strict, yet simple: You must be saved. Inside the city are the famous "streets of gold" (see expression "streets of gold"); in fact, everything in it is made of pure gold. The city will actually descend from heaven and be placed on earth by God himself at his return. New Jerusalem will be the most magnificent sight you will ever see outside of Jesus Christ.

New Jerusalem is not symbolic or figurative, for one of the city's main purposes is to house every believer's mansion that Jesus talked about in John chapter fourteen. Even Abraham, the patriarch of the Old Testament, was said to be looking for it according to Hebrews 11:10: "For he looked for a city which hath foundations, whose builder and maker *is* God." As you can see, when God builds a city, he goes all out.

play the fool

> ¶ Then said Saul, I have sinned: return, my son David: for I will no more do thee harm, because my soul was precious in thine eyes this day: behold, I have **played the fool**, and have erred exceedingly. (1 Samuel 26:21)

"Everybody plays the fool, sometimes. There's no exception to the rule." Remember these words from the old pop song? King Saul of Israel said he "played the fool" after he had been pursuing David to kill him. At the same time, however, Saul was being threatened by his enemies, which gave David a chance to kill King Saul. David declined to do so, and this action convicted Saul who admitted he "erred and played the fool" about trying to kill David.

Foolishness in scripture is always associated with wickedness. "The foolishness of man perverteth his way: and his heart fretteth against the LORD." According to Jesus, the wisest man to ever live even tried foolishness: "I applied mine heart to know, and to search, and to seek out wisdom, and the reason *of things*, and to know the wickedness of folly, even of foolishness *and* madness" (Ecclesiastes 7:25). Man likes to think foolishness is cute, but surprise, surprise, God thinks differently.

powers that be

> LET every soul be subject unto the higher powers. For there is no power but of God: **the powers that be** are ordained of God. (Romans 13:1)

We hear this often in reference to our bosses at work or anyone who is in charge and makes the rules. "The powers that be" has particular relevance to governmental leaders whom the Bible says are "ordained of God" no matter who they are.

That means everyone from Bill Clinton to Adolf Hitler has been put in power by God. God places these people in positions of power for his own reasons, whether it is to punish a nation and cause it to repent or bless a nation for it faithfulness. God will ordain whom he wants regardless of our campaigning or political maneuvering. Thus, Jesus can't be labeled a Republican, Democrat, Fascist, or Socialist because he has appointed all these at one time or another.

promised land

> By faith he sojourned in the **land of promise**, as *in* a strange country, dwelling in tabernacles with Isaac and Jacob, the heirs with him of the same promise: (Hebrews 11:9)

If you want to know the cause of the Middle East peace problem, you need look no further than the promise of land (promised land) that God made to Abraham in Genesis 15:18: "In the same day the LORD made a covenant with Abram, saying, Unto thy seed have I given this land, from the river of Egypt unto the great river, the river Euphrates."

The problem stems from the fact that Abraham had his firstborn son Ishmael through his maid Hagar, but Isaac came from his wife Sarah. As was the law, the firstborn son inherits most of his father's property. God recognized Isaac as the only legitimate heir by the fact that Isaac is called the firstborn by God even though he physically wasn't. Thus, the descendants of Isaac, the Jews, and the descendants of

Ishmael, the Arabs, fight to this very day over who owns the birthright to Abraham's promised land.

The Arabs' contention that Ishmael should be the heir is clearly refuted in such passages as Genesis 21:12: "And God said unto Abraham, Let it not be grievous in thy sight because of the lad, and because of thy bondwoman; in all that Sarah hath said unto thee, hearken unto her voice; for in Isaac shall thy seed be called." If the Arabs don't recognize the Bible as their authority, that's not God or the Jews' problem. God can give the promised land to whom he chooses, and he chose Israel and the descendants of Abraham.

prophet without honor

> And they were offended in him. But Jesus said unto them, **A prophet is not without honour**, save in his own country, and in his own house. (Matthew 13:57)

A prophet without honor is one that doesn't get the recognition he deserves, especially from his own country or town. Jesus said all of Israel's prophets received dishonor and even death at the hands of their own countrymen, and that same fate would not pass by Jesus Christ who was the ultimate prophet without honor.

The context of this discussion involved Jesus' teaching in the synagogue and the people's astonishment at the wisdom he showed. In Matthew 13:55-6, they asked the following: "Is not this the carpenter's son? Is not his mother called Mary? and his brethren, James, and Joses, and Simon, and Judas? And his sisters, are they not all with us? Whence then hath this *man* all these things?"

Jesus had sisters and brothers? Unbeknownst to many, he definitely did, but you don't hear that talked about, do you? The reason for this conspiracy of silence is that it destroys the myth of Mary still being a virgin, which she is not. It is not right to designate Jesus' mother as the Virgin Mary today. Exposing this heresy to the mainline churches today will definitely make you a "prophet without honor" in their eyes.

pull out of the fire

> And others save with fear, **pulling *them* out of the fire**; hating even the garment spotted by the flesh. (Jude 23)

Rescuing someone from a hostile or dangerous situation could also be called "pulling out of the fire." As used in the word of God, "pulling out of the fire" means delivering an individual from the impending sentence of hell by helping them to get saved. Even though the sinner is not in the fire of hell, God implies the sinner is so close that he should be pulled out of it.

Once an individual is in hell, that's one fire he won't get pulled out of. Christians take on many roles, and helping lost sinners by pulling them out of the fire makes the Christian a true fire fighter.

put it on my tab

> If he hath wronged thee, or oweth *thee* ought, **put that on mine account**; (Philemon 18)

"Put it on my tab," we like to say. Although there were no charge cards in Paul's day, he was willing to have charged to his account any wrongdoings his friend Onesimus might have committed. This action demonstrated the heart of the gospel: the innocent willing to suffer for the guilty.

Most of us have a hard enough time being willing to suffer for our own guilt much less the guilt of others. The bill that each one of us owes for sins is one tab that can't be paid by us, the debtors. The fact that Jesus took on all the sin of the world at the cross showed that he paid the biggest one time bill ever accumulated, for we all put it on his "tab," and he was more than willing to pay it.

Drinks are still on the house today: "But whosoever drinketh of the water that I shall give him shall never thirst; but the water that I shall give him shall be in him a well of water springing up into everlasting life." If we don't put our sins on his tab, we definitely don't want it on ours, for he won't accept payment of any kind except his own blood.

put words in someone's mouth

And come to the king, and speak on this manner unto him. So Joab **put the words in her mouth**. (2 Samuel 14:30

When we tell someone what we think he or she is trying to say, that individual will inevitably fire back and say, "Don't put words into my mouth." In biblical usage, Joab, an Israelite army captain, is said to have "put words into the mouth" of a woman named Tekoah. Joab wanted to use this woman to deceive King David by telling her words to say to the king.

Putting words into people's mouths is precisely what God did to all the prophets who uttered or wrote his words as recorded in our Bible: "As for me, this *is* my covenant with them, saith the LORD; My spirit that *is* upon thee, and my words which I have put in thy mouth, shall not depart out of thy mouth, nor out of the mouth of thy seed, nor out of the mouth of thy seed's seed, saith the LORD, from henceforth and for ever."

For us to change the words that he has meticulously placed in our Bible would make us guilty of putting words in his mouth. If there's anyone that you don't want to do that to, it's Jesus Christ. He created the universe, so he's quite capable of giving us a book that doesn't need correcting. He gave us his words so they could "be put in our mouths."

put your hand to the plow

And Jesus said unto him, No man, having **put his hand to the plough**, and looking back, is fit for the kingdom of God. (Luke 9:62)

This is another of Jesus' so-called "hard sayings." Some will misinterpret this quote to mean that if we as believers go astray, we are "not fit." What Jesus was teaching was if we are double-minded and not sure if we want to choose him or not, we are then "not fit." Having second thoughts about believing in God would be the equivalent analogy.

put your life in someone's hands

For he did **put his life in his hand**, and slew the Philistine, and the LORD wrought a great salvation for all Israel: thou sawest *it*, and didst rejoice: wherefore then wilt thou sin against innocent blood, to slay David without a cause? (1 Samuel 19:5)

Jonathan, the son of King Saul, tried to persuade his father not to kill David, for David, it said, had "put his life in his hand" by slaying Goliath the giant, thus saving Israel. Jonathan, then, helped to save David's life because he convinced his father not to kill David.

We usually speak of "putting our lives into someone else's hands" when, in a potentially life threatening situation, we place our faith in doctors, lawyers, mechanics, and others who could slip up and actually cause us to lose our lives. The same people that have a hard time putting their faith in God don't think twice to do the same with people they don't even know.

Q

quick and the dead

> I CHARGE *thee* therefore before God, and the Lord Jesus Christ, who shall judge **the quick and the dead** at his appearing and his kingdom; (2 Timothy 4:1)

A very popular title of books and movies (see appendix), "the quick and the dead" signifies the living and the dead whom Jesus will judge at his coming. Though he's judging the quick, it's not the swift he's talking about. The word "quick" used to mean living as well as swift.

Whether a criminal is living or dead obviously affects if he can get out of paying for his crime. You can't bring a dead man to justice; however, Jesus can and will. He will raise all the dead and judge them, and then cast many of the same back down into hell. Death does not exempt you from your crimes as far as Jesus is concerned.

R

race is not to the swift

¶ I returned, and saw under the sun, that **the race _is_ not to the swift**, nor the battle to the strong, neither yet bread to the wise, nor yet riches to men of understanding, nor yet favour to men of skill; but time and chance happeneth to them all. (Ecclesiastes 9:11)

Remember the theme of the tortoise and the hare fable? That theme is the meaning of the biblical saying "the race is not to the swift." The winner is not always the fastest, smartest, or strongest, but he is the one who is the wisest and most persistent. It is ironic that this was the finding of King Solomon, who was the smartest and strongest king who ever lived.

Notice that we are indeed in a "race," not a rat race as the world would have us believe, but a race that is to be run with patience according to Hebrews 12:1. The Christian's race makes all who run in it a winner, for the first place prize is Jesus Christ.

The apostle Paul used the very same language when he wrote to the church at Phillipi: "I press toward the mark for the prize of the high calling of God in Christ Jesus" (see expression "eyes on the prize"). It's not who has the most toys that wins, but who has the right prize.

reap what you sow

Be not deceived; God is not mocked: for **whatsoever a man soweth, that shall he also reap**. (Galatians 6:7)

"What goes around comes around," and "You'll get what's coming to you" are equivalent expressions that have to do with a person getting what he deserves for some untoward actions he has committed. The Bible acknowledges the laws of nature, for just as the farmer gets what he plants, the same is true in the spiritual world. The right soil, the right fertilizer, and plenty of water will produce a good crop as well as a good Christian. You can't fool Mother Nature, and you definitely can't fool Father God.

right in your own eyes

> The way of a fool *is* **right in his own eyes**: but he that hearkeneth unto counsel *is* wise.   (Proverbs 12:15)

One characteristic of a fool, according to the Bible, is that he thinks he's always right. Since he's only right in his own eyes, he accepts no other arguments. If you are right in your eyes, then you don't consider other viewpoints.

Christians will often be labeled as "arrogant" and "right in their own eyes," and this expression is used against those believers who are certain of their beliefs and who will not waver. Those who engage in this activity try to convince believers that intelligence these days is measured not by how much black and white you see in issues, but how much gray you perceive. If you are certain about anything or believe in any absolutes, you are construed as "narrow minded" and not "objective" enough.

The Christian should remember that what he believes is not true because he believes it, but it is true only because it is in the scriptures. Thus, the argument is not whether the Christian is right or wrong (that is an intended smoke screen); it is whether the Bible is right or wrong. God is the only one who is truly "right in his own eyes," and to question anything he says will make you "wrong in his own eyes."

ripe old age

> And Gideon the son of Joash died in **a good old age**, and was buried in the sepulchre of Joash his father, in Ophrah of the Abi-ezrites. (Judges 8:32)

"Only the good die young" goes the popular saying. To live long, or to a ripe old age, is not for the evil only, but also for the good. One of the Ten Commandments promises that children will live long if they obey their parents: "¶ Honour thy father and thy mother: that thy days may be long upon the land which the LORD thy God giveth thee" (Exodus 20:12).

No wonder we have so many children dying so young today—nobody obeys their parents! Parents needn't worry too much about discipline problems if their kids take this warning seriously.

rise and fall of...

And Simeon blessed them, and said unto Mary his mother, Behold, this *child* is set for **the fall and rising again of** many in Israel; and for a sign which shall be spoken against; (Luke 2:34)

This saying is reversed in modern usage, and finds its place in the titles of many books and movies. David Bowie entitled one of his best-selling albums *The Rise and Fall of Ziggy Stardust and the Spiders from Mars*. Many famous achievers are known for rising to the top and then falling out of the limelight.

God speaks of Israel falling first and then rising again in the last days to a prominence she had never before attained. This is exactly what happened with the country of Israel. It fell to the Romans in A.D. 70 and was completely annihilated to the point of losing its national borders and ceasing to exist as a country. Almost 1,900 years later, Israel, through the providence of God, became a nation again in 1948, despite the surrounding countries trying to make sure it didn't. God is now readying the world for the rising again of Israel to fulfill his plan for the end times. For more on this late-breaking story, consult the local listings in your Bible guide.

rise and shine

> **ARISE, shine** for thy light is come, and the glory of the LORD is risen upon thee. (Isaiah 60:1)

Used regularly as the morning trumpet song in the army, "rise and shine" is the universal language for "get up and get out of bed." The Bible says we are to "rise and shine" because our light has come (Jesus). Jesus does indeed cause our faces to shine.

You can tell the difference between a child of God and a child of the Devil by the shine that God puts on their faces. In Phillipians 2:15, God says, "That ye may be blameless and harmless, the sons of God, without rebuke, in the midst of a crooked and perverse nation, among whom ye shine as lights in the world."

The wicked have their own shine as well and try to shine without the Son, so discernment is necessary to distinguish them from the true Christian. Since Jesus is "the light of the world," any other light is false and is like comparing artificial light to the light of the sun—there is no comparison. Only the Son makes us truly shine.

root and branch

> FOR, behold, the day cometh, that shall burn as an oven; and all the proud, yea, and all that do wickedly, shall be stubble: and the day that cometh shall burn them up, saith the LORD of hosts, that it shall leave them neither **root nor branch**. (Malachi 4:1)

The Bible says the wicked shall be burned "root and branch" at the return of Jesus Christ, making reference not only to the burning of their bodies but also the burning of their souls, thus destroying body and soul, or root and branch.

Anyone knows that to kill a weed you just can't chop it down; you have to destroy the root. The same goes for sinners, who, by the way, are also called "weeds" or "tares" by Jesus, the real exterminator. He'll weed out all the tares that are trying to take root in your life.

root of all evil

For the love of money is **the root of all evil**: which while some coveted after, they have erred from the faith, and pierced themselves through with many sorrows. (1 Timothy 6:10)

Quite often, this expression is misquoted as saying, "Money is the root of all evil," thus changing its entire meaning. It is "the <u>love</u> of money" that is the "root of all evil." If you ever want to find out the cause of some corruption, "follow the money trail" as some would say.

Despite its tendency for abuse, the need for money is what keeps many unbelievers somewhat obedient to the dictates of society, i.e., holding a job, being responsible, etc. If people didn't have to earn a living, think how much these people would corrupt themselves and the world because they no longer have to get along in order to survive. We should be thankful for the need to earn money.

Versions other than the King James translate this scripture as "<u>a</u> root of all kinds of evil." There is quite a difference between the words "a" and "the" and the words "all" and "all kinds." The very meaning of this scripture is exemplified in the twisting of the scripture itself in the newer versions. "The love of money" is precisely what caused Bible correctors to change the verse's harsh statement of "the root of all evil" to the more popular and better selling ($) "a root of all kinds of evil."

"Speak unto us smooth things, prophesy deceits" (Isaiah 30:10) said the people unto the false prophets. People will choose being lied to over hearing the truth of the Bible. The Bible would agree with Jack Nicholson who said in *A Few Good Men*, "You can't handle the truth."

rooted and grounded in...

That Christ may dwell in your hearts by faith; that ye, being **rooted and grounded in** love, May be able to comprehend with all saints what *is* the breadth, and length, and depth, and height; (Ephesians 3:17-18)

When you know something backwards and forwards and know it like the back of your hand, you were probably rooted and grounded in it by much study or experience. Unfortunately, some are so rooted and grounded in false love and false doctrine, it takes a lot of uprooting and tearing down to occur before a new plant can be planted.

root (heart) of the matter

But ye should say, Why persecute we him, seeing **the root of the matter** is found in me? (Job 19:28)

Trying to get to the bottom of something is akin to finding out "the root of the matter." As used in the scriptures, the phrase "the root of the matter" is employed by Job when his so-called friends blamed Job for his own suffering. Job said that "the root of the matter," or the cause of his suffering, was his friends. Job denied their accusation, and rightly so, for God himself acknowledged Job as a perfect man.

Job was a fine example of the phrase "with friends like these, who needs enemies." Job's so-called friends were nothing but wolves in sheep's clothing (see expression "wolves in sheep's clothing") who manipulated the word of God just enough to confuse the average man. Job saw through it, though, and did not fall for their false praise and false condemnation cloaked in the guise of religion. The Bible is an excellent tool for helping you get to "the root of the matter."

ruin of someone

For he sacrificed unto the gods of Damascus, which smote him: and he said, Because the gods of the kings of Syria help them, *therefore* will I sacrifice to them, that they may help me. But they **were the ruin of him**, and of all Israel. (2 Chronicles 28:23)

If this isn't the epitome of modern day utilitarianism ("If it works, use it" philosophy), nothing is. King Ahaz thought if the gods of the kings of Syria helped the Syrians, they should work for him also, so he worshipped them.

Doesn't this sound all too familiar? "Why don't we," some say, "take what works for the world and put it to use in the church? If it was successful for them, we can make it successful for us; only, let's modify it somewhat and make it look more church-like." A good rule of thumb to remember: If the world thinks highly of something, God doesn't, because "that which is highly esteemed among men is abomination in the sight of God" (Luke 16:15). When's the last time you heard that verse quoted? You probably won't hear it because the teaching itself could be "the ruin of someone."

rule with an iron hand

And out of his mouth goeth a sharp sword, that with it he should smite the nations: and he shall **rule them with a rod of iron**: and he treadeth the winepress of the fierceness and wrath of Almighty God. (Revelation 19:15)

Most often, this expression applies to a harsh, strict boss or political leader who severely punishes disobedience. This same meaning turns up in the book of Revelation in regard to the reign of Jesus Christ who it says will also rule with an iron hand or "rod of iron" as scripture puts it.

Naturally, Jesus will have the power no other leader has had to crush any opposition to his rule, and he won't need a military to do it. "Every knee shall bow" to the King of Kings in fear or in worship. Jesus will make Hitler look like a Boy Scout, for he will be the fiercest dictator the world has ever known to those who oppose him, but a good dictator to those who love him.

run for your lives

And it came to pass, when they had brought them forth abroad, that he said, **Escape for thy life**; look not behind thee, neither stay thou in all the plain; escape to the mountain, lest thou be consumed. (Genesis 19:17)

The destruction of Sodom and Gomorrah for their iniquity was delayed mercifully by God until God's angels took Lot and his family out. Lot was told to "escape for thy life" or "run for your life" as we say today. God brought out Lot even though Lot didn't want to go according to the scriptures. Lot actually enjoyed some of the goings-on in Sodom.

Despite Lot's worldly ways, God still calls Lot a "just man" in 2 Peter 2:7 even though it also said Lot was "vexed with the filthy conversation of the wicked." This "filthy conversation" is not referring to his speech, but his lifestyle, as "conversation" has changed in meaning.

A doctrine like this runs contrary to the teaching that a Christian doesn't sin like the world does. It also goes against the teaching that you can lose your salvation if you're "bad" enough. You can't get much more worldly than what Lot was doing. He hung around in Sodom and Gomorrah and was living it up with its infamous inhabitants, yet God proclaimed Lot to be a good man, not because of his actions, but because of his belief.

S

safe and sound

> And he said unto him, Thy brother is come; and thy father hath killed the fatted calf, because he hath received him **safe and sound**. (Luke 15:27)

From the story of the Prodigal Son comes the cliché "safe and sound." It refers, as most already know, to the wayward son who returned "safe and sound" to his father after the son realized the error of his ways.

This famous account has provided us with other common expressions such as "lost and found," "kill the fatted calf," and "riotous living." One reason for this story's popularity is that it parallels the lives of many families who have children that rebel and run away from their parents to live it up. Later, the children realize that the party lifestyle will make them end up like the Prodigal Son—broke, hungry, and lost.

Jesus, like the father in the account, will not stop those who want to pursue this way of living, but he will always be waiting for those who realize they need him. Like the father of the Prodigal Son, Jesus also will have a huge dinner party for his children, and that party is known as the "marriage supper of the lamb." It is not known whether he will also be serving "fatted calf."

salt of the earth

> ¶ Ye are **the salt of the earth**: but if the salt have lost his savour, wherewith shall it be salted? it is thenceforth good for nothing, but to be cast out, and to be trodden under foot of men. (Matthew 5:13)

You can't give a finer compliment to another than to describe him as "the salt of the earth," i.e., the best or noblest of people. Christians, according to Jesus, are the "salt of the earth," preserving, as salt does, the virtues of God and applying them to a world that is decaying. Because Jesus distinguished Christians as the "salt of the earth," it would be biblically incorrect to call anyone else the same title.

Salt, by the way, is not bad for you as most would have you believe. Jesus said "Salt is good" in this passage, so who are you going to believe, Jesus or everyone else? Go ahead and reach for that shaker of salt; you have God's blessing.

saving grace

> Even when we were dead in sins, hath quickened us together with Christ, (by **grace ye are saved**;) (Ephesians 2:5)

Notice that it didn't say in Ephesians "by grace are ye saved through water baptism, speaking in tongues, doing more good than bad, or the Eucharist." Jesus saves all by himself and doesn't need any help from any of the above because he doesn't share his glory with anyone.

The word "save" has become so adulterated with all the world wanting to "save the whales, save the trees, save the ozone layer, and save money" that saving your soul doesn't have the impact it used to. That's just one more thing we need to save.

A "saving grace" as it is used today speaks of a particular quality of a person or thing that keeps it from being all bad. Biblically speaking, no unbeliever has any saving grace because his whole soul is corrupt. That's why he needs the literal saving grace of Jesus.

say the word, just

> The centurion answered and said, Lord, I am not worthy that thou shouldest come under my roof: but **speak the word only**, and my servant shall be healed. (Matthew 8:8)

Jesus said he saw no greater example of faith than did his own disciples. "Just say the word" means a person is ready and willing to do whatever the other desires.

Like the centurion, the military man and the Christian have a lot in common. Both recognize the need for authority and obedience to it, and both are soldiers who should be prepared for war at anytime.

scales (blinders) fell from your eyes

And immediately there **fell from his eyes as it had been scales**: and he received sight forthwith, and arose, and was baptized. (Acts 9:18)

After Paul literally saw the light (see expression "see the light") of Jesus on his way to Damascus, he was temporarily blinded for three days. A disciple named Ananias was instructed by God to lay hands on Paul. He did so, and Paul received his sight back with the "scales" falling from his eyes. "Blinders on the eyes" is the modern equivalent, but it means the same—something that is keeping you from seeing the whole picture.

Jesus describes all that are lost as "blind" and "deaf." Helen Keller's condition of being deaf, dumb, and blind would be an apt description of all those who don't know Jesus. Imagine being unable to see or hear, and you will understand how God sees each of those who reject him, just as Jesus made mention when he said, "Therefore speak I unto them in parables: because they seeing see not; and hearing they hear not, neither do they understand" (Matthew 13:13). We are all spiritually handicapped at one time or another.

scum of the earth (filth of the world)

Being defamed, we intreat: we are made as **the filth of the world**, *and are* the offscouring of all things unto this day. (1 Corinthians 4:13)

Anytime a Christian wants to get respect from the world, he should consider the fact that the world thinks he is the scum of the earth or "filth of the world" as the Bible puts it. If this is not the case, either the secular person is lying, or the so-called Christian isn't acting like a Christian, for the "bloodthirsty hate the upright" according to the Bible (Proverbs 29:10). This idea is akin to the old adage, "A man is known by his enemies."

Yes, Christians are relegated to "scum"—quite a contrast to the modern "Christian" who longs for the world's approval and tries to incorporate the world's lifestyle into his own. That is why when this truth is told to so-called believers, many don't believe it. Their argument, however, is with the Bible, not those who point this out to them. If you mind being considered "scum," Christianity may not be for you. Wear your scum badge with honor.

see eye to eye

> The watchmen shall lift up the voice; with the voice together shall they sing: for they shall **see eye to eye**, when the LORD shall bring again Zion. (Isaiah 52:8)

Agreeing with each other and sharing a common understanding could be deemed "seeing eye to eye." The Bible prophesied of a time when God's people would see eye to eye because Jesus would be reigning in Zion and everything would be right. This expression is usually used in the negative sense when it is said people "don't see eye to eye."

People don't like to look each other in the eyes if they don't like one another. There's something about the eyes that reveal a person's heart; hence, the expression, "The eyes are the windows of the soul." Those that don't want you to see their eyes may be doing so in order for you not to see their soul. That's usually not a pretty sight anyway.

see the light

He will deliver his soul from going into the pit, and his life shall **see the light**. (Job 33:28)

Job's friend Elihu gave his prescription for attaining righteousness by saying that if any man says he has sinned, God will rescue him from hell and he will "see the light." To "see the light" is to fully grasp the meaning or importance of a matter. In the biblical sense, this expression is used when one sees the light of Jesus, the light of the world.

Many use this expression jokingly or in sarcasm to mock those who have been saved, because to them, others supposedly "saw the light" and got saved. Those that really have seen the light shouldn't use such language so flippantly, for God's saving of your soul shouldn't become the butt of a joke or be compared to any other situation.

see the light of day, not

Let the stars of the twilight thereof be dark; let it look for light, but *have* none; **neither let it see the dawning of the day**: (Job 3:9)

Telling someone that he won't "see the light of day" is a warning that he is about to be incarcerated or prevented from living normally usually because of something that person did. It could also mean something won't come to fruition or come to pass; hence, it won't see the light of day that is coming.

Job was cursing the day he was born for all his suffering, and the Bible says he desired for the stars not to see the "dawning of the day." Job questioned why God gave him wisdom: "*Why is light given* to a man whose way is hid, and whom God hath hedged in?" (Job 3:23).

That is a good question. Why does God give wisdom to those people who are "hid" and "hedged" in? The reason is that God uses the foolish things of this world to confound the wise. He also is a God that hides his truth from the wicked: "Verily thou *art* a God that hidest thyself, O God of Israel, the Saviour" (Isaiah 45:15).

You could say God plays a little hide and seek; he hides, and you seek. God has some good hiding places, and it takes a lot of seeking to find him. You may question the fact that God hides from man, but man does the same thing. Read the account of Adam and Eve, and notice that Adam tried to hide from God after the eating of the fruit. God will always win every game of "hide and seek," for "the eyes of the LORD *are* in every place, beholding the evil and the good."

see to it

When Pilate saw that he could prevail nothing, but *that* rather a tumult was made, he took water, and washed *his* hands before the multitude, saying, I am innocent of the blood of this just person: **see ye *to it*.** (Matthew 27:24)

Pilate didn't want to take responsibility for the fate of Jesus especially after the uproar of the crowd, so he "washed his hands" of the matter (see expression "washed his hands"). He told the Jews to "see ye to it" and handle the matter themselves. The Jews saw to it and crucified Jesus, despite the fact that Pilate declared him a "just person."

This incident exemplified democracy in action, the inevitable result of which is mob rule. Since democracy is the rule of the people, if the will of the majority is corrupt (and it is quite often), so will be the government. There are other examples of the democratic process in the Bible, and almost every time democracy is practiced, the people choose a corrupt leader or go against the will of God. Two prime examples of this are the choosing of Saul as King of Israel and Aaron as leader of the Israelites. Both of these actions led to the corruption of Israel.

A democracy is no more spiritually sanctioned by God than a dictatorship though Americans like to think our form of government is the godliest. We also like to think that the majority always knows what is right. The majority in this country passes all kinds of ungodly laws. That only goes to show that the majority of people's hearts are wicked, not that the majority vote makes things right.

seek, and ye shall find

¶ Ask, and it shall be given you; **seek, and ye shall find**; knock, and it shall be opened unto you: (Matthew 7:7)

A popular quotation as well as biblical expression, "seek and ye shall find" finds itself used by Jesus in his Sermon on the Mount speech when he tells the multitudes to "ask," "seek," and "knock." Door-to-door salesmen shouldn't have any trouble relating to this command.

Seeking God is no different, but God knows when you've found him, even if you don't. People will often claim they have tried to seek God or find the truth, but they end up frustrated. This sounds like a noble effort until you realize they are lying or are deceived, for God says you will find him when you seek him with your whole heart and nothing less: "And ye shall seek me, and find *me*, when ye shall search for me with all your heart" (Jeremiah 29:13).

This is the true meaning of "seek, and ye shall find." It's really very simple: if you haven't found God, you haven't searched for him with your whole heart, even though you think you have done so.

separate the sheep from the goats

And before him shall be gathered all nations: and he shall **separate** them one from another, as a shepherd divideth *his* **sheep from the goats**: (Matthew 25:32)

To organize or put things or people into different groups is to "separate the sheep from the goats." When Jesus separates the sheep from the goats, he will be distinguishing between the believers and the wicked, the believers being the sheep, and the goats being the wicked.

One reason that you always see goats associated with evil and sheep with good could be this parable told by

Jesus. Another tidbit possibly derived from this account is the association between left-handed and evil and right-handed and good. The sheep are put on Jesus' right hand and the goats on his left. Don't worry, though, all you left-handed sinners, God can still save your soul. You're no more wicked than a right-hander.

sell one's soul

> For what is a man profited, if he shall gain the whole world, and lose his own soul? or what shall a man give in **exchange for his soul**? (Matthew 16:26)

This passage has been made famous by the story of the doctor who sells his soul to the Devil for worldly gain. When someone sells his soul today, it could also speak of selling out or giving in to whatever desires he has to the point of forsaking everything else.

Jesus asked what is worth abandoning the soul for, yet that is the question everyone is faced with when getting saved. If something is worth more to you than everlasting life, then you will never receive God's gift. Whatever is keeping you from God is something that you may have already "sold your soul" for.

set your heart on something

> What *is* man, that thou shouldest magnify him? and that thou shouldest **set thine heart upon him**? (Job 7:17)

The only thing that God has set his heart on is man according to Job. "What is man, that thou art mindful of him? and the son of man, that thou visitest him?" asked David in the book of Psalms.

One of the greatest wonders is why God is interested in man in the first place. God doesn't need man for anything, despite some of the prevailing heresies of the day, which say that God needed someone to show his affection to. God got along just fine for billions of years without man. The fact that

God became a man is one answer why he is mindful of him. God is forever bonded to the human race by that one unspeakable act of being "manifest in the flesh" (1 Timothy 3:16).

set your teeth on edge

> In those days they shall say no more, The fathers have eaten a sour grape, and the children's **teeth are set on edge**. (Jeremiah 31:29)

Did you ever notice that our teeth really do line up on edge when we are nervous, anxious, mad, etc.? The Bible reserves this phrase for those who have committed so much sin that their impending punishment is actually causing their teeth to be on edge. This expression is similar to another that occurs in the wicked (see "gnash your teeth").

shake the dust off your feet

> And whosoever shall not receive you, nor hear your words, when ye depart out of that house or city, **shake off the dust of your feet**. (Matthew 10:14)

Jesus' way of telling us not to get down when others won't receive our testimony of him was to "shake off the dust of your feet." This saying is comparable to the expression "shake it off," which refers to someone ridding himself of some undesirable notion or feeling.

Many Christians sometimes feel that if others aren't accepting their testimony, somehow, something they did was wrong. Christians should expect that most would reject the truth. It is when most are accepting that they should realize that something they are doing is probably compromising the gospel, for "broad *is* the way, that leadeth to destruction, and many there be that go in thereat."

shout it from the housetops

> What I tell you in darkness, *that* speak ye in light: and what ye hear in the ear, *that* **preach ye upon the housetops**. (Matthew 10:27)

Getting excited about something and announcing it to the world at every opportunity is the meaning of this expression today. Jesus told his disciples to preach the gospel from the housetops, if need be, to further his message.

Back then, there were no loudspeakers and megaphones to proclaim his word, so a housetop was one option. Today, we have a choice: housetops, megaphones, televisions, etc. The world today will treat you as some type of nut to do things like this, but Jesus expected it as a normal course of action in the Christian life. Guess that makes him a "nut," too.

signs of the times

> He answered and said unto them, When it is evening, ye say, *It will be* fair weather: for the sky is red. And in the morning, *It will be* foul weather to day: for the sky is red and lowring. O *ye* hypocrites, ye can discern the face of the sky; but can ye not *discern* **the signs of the times**? (Matthew 16:2-3)

Any characteristic that is indicative of modern day society, especially if it's a negative one, is called a "sign of the times." Jesus said the Pharisees were able to read the sky and predict the weather, but they were unable to read the signs of the times. Jesus was pointing out the hypocrisy of keeping up with all the changing weather signs but ignoring the other signs that God gives a nation on the brink of judgment.

Even the weather itself is a sign of the end times, as Jesus himself spoke of the times just before his return by saying, "fearful sights, and great signs shall there be from heaven" (Luke 21:11), "signs in the sun, and in the moon, and in the stars; and upon the earth distress of nations, with perplexity; the sea and the waves roaring" (Luke 21:25). The expression, "How's the weather?" is a little more involved than you might think.

sing someone's praises

> Then believed they his words; they **sang his praise**. (Psalms 106:12)

It should be obvious to any Christian that the use of this phrase was used for God only though the world likes to use it for its own. "Singing someone's praises" speaks of lauding and extolling a person greatly.

sink into your ears

> Let these sayings **sink down into your ears**: for the Son of man shall be delivered into the hands of men. (Luke 9:44)

One of the many fitting expressions Jesus used was this one when he was speaking to his disciples about his death. He didn't want there to be any misunderstanding of what he was saying, so he told them to let his sayings "sink down into your ears."

Although Jesus emphasized his impending death, they still didn't realize what he was talking about. It just didn't get into their "thick skulls" as we would say. As hardheaded as we are, God's words can still penetrate even the thickest of skulls.

sins of the fathers

> And he walked in all **the sins of his father**, which he had done before him: and his heart was not perfect with the LORD his God, as the heart of David his father. (1 Kings 15:3)

The evil deeds of our ancestors are known as the "sins of the fathers." Though parents are responsible for the way they raise their kids, kids are responsible for their own actions as well. In 1st Kings, Abijam reigns in wickedness like his father Rehoboam, but just because his father was wicked doesn't mean that it was inevitable that his son Abijam would be, too.

All over the land, you hear children blaming their parents for all the problems the kids are having. While it is perfectly true that parents influence their kids negatively, this notion that kids aren't responsible for their actions because of the way they were raised is nonsense. Even though there are sincere cases of child abuse and so forth, this does not excuse any sins of the child.

Society would like to blame anything but the person who commits the act. It's no different than the "Devil made me do it" mentality that is sweeping this country today. "Don't blame me; blame the parents, the schools, my genes, television, peer pressure,"—anything but the real cause—the child's evil heart.

sit in judgment on

A king that **sitteth in** the throne of **judgment** scattereth away all evil with his eyes. (Proverbs 20:8)

If there's one scripture everybody knows, it's the one that says "judge not." If there was ever a scripture that was yanked out of context, it was this one. The minute you sit in judgment on a matter, the world will attack you and try to justify their attack biblically by quoting this "judge not" phrase from the book of Matthew.

The Christian that knows his Bible will not fall for this trickery, for he knows that he is commanded to judge all things: "But he that is spiritual judgeth all things, yet he himself is judged of no man (1 Corinthians 2:15). If we are not to judge, then we couldn't distinguish between right and wrong, Christian and unbeliever, etc. The Christian's love actually grows when his judgment increases: "And this I pray, that your love may abound yet more and more in knowledge and in all judgment" (Phillipians 1:9). *Love itself* is demonstrated by sound judgment, not the avoidance of it.

When the scripture says "judge not, that ye be not judged, you never hear that second half of the verse that says, "For with what judgment ye judge, ye shall be judged"; thus, it is taken out of context. The Bible is not telling you not to judge, only that, if you do, you will be judged with the same judgment. That is a far cry from "Don't judge."

Think about this: When the world tells you that you shouldn't judge, they themselves are judging your commandment to judge. That is what is meant in the scriptures when its says the wicked will be "speaking lies in hypocrisy."

sitting on top of the world

> *It is* he that **sitteth upon the circle of the earth**, and the inhabitants thereof *are* as grasshoppers; that stretcheth out the heavens as a curtain, and spreadeth them out as a tent to dwell in: (Isaiah 40:22)

When you've got it made and are deemed successful, this qualifies you as "sitting on top of the world." Not surprisingly, this scripture applies literally to God and God alone of whom the Bible says that it is he only who "sitteth upon the circle of the earth" (Isaiah 40:22).

What do you know; the Bible says the earth is round. You mean scientists didn't "discover" this till thousands of years later? Maybe people ought to read this archaic, antiquated book a little more carefully. They might find out God's book is a few steps ahead of the scientists.

so be it

> And she said, According unto your words, **so *be* it**. And she sent them away, and they departed: and she bound the scarlet line in the window. (Joshua 2:21)

After Rahab hid the spies in her house and lied about it to their pursuers, she made a covenant with the spies and was promised protection by them in the upcoming battle. The book of Hebrews said she received them by faith, so some commentators wonder how her lying was considered faith. It wasn't. The fact that she received the spies was by faith, not the lying about it. So be it.

sour grapes

> What mean ye, that ye use this proverb concerning the land of Israel, saying, The fathers have eaten **sour grapes**, and the children's teeth are set on edge? (Ezekiel 18:2)

We all know the feeling of eating a sour grape, and this is also the feeling of the Israelite fathers who were said to have eaten "sour grapes," meaning they were bitter and upset. This meaning differs somewhat from the modern one of pretending not to want something you can't have.

The Bible mentions that this was a proverb at the time of Ezekiel (594 B.C.), so this was an established proverb long before it showed up in Aesop's fables of which many claim the phrase came from. It seems some people have a case of "sour grapes" when it comes to recognizing where these expressions originated.

spare the rod, (spoil the child)

> He that **spareth his rod** hateth his son: but he that loveth him chasteneth him betimes. (Proverbs 13:24)

In this day and age of lax discipline, those parents who believe their Bible would do well to take heed to this admonition. "Spoiling the child" was not part of the original quote, but was added in place of the part most want to ignore. If you spare the rod according to the Bible, that means you hate your children. Wow! What a 180-degree turn against child rearing (no pun intended) that is!

Child advocates constantly harp on how spanking is bad for your child. Scripture refutes that notion and adds that neglecting to do so shows you don't care enough about your child. God never prescribed "removing privileges," "time-out," or any other of these ineffective, psychological, anti-biblical methods for punishing your child. He never prescribed beating your child up either, but that's what everyone screams about to justify their opposition to it.

sparks are going to fly

Yet man is born unto trouble, as the **sparks fly** upward. (Job 5:7)

You hear the expression "Sparks are gonna fly" whenever a situation is getting ready to be hostile between two parties. Man, according to Eliphaz the Temanite in the book of Job, is "born unto trouble." Perhaps this is also an allusion to the common adage "born to be wild" (see appendix).

The Bible student knows that all are born to be wild, not just the overtly rebellious we see around us. Scripture states that all men are "born unto trouble," we are all rebels and "natural born liars" (see Psalm 58:3).

speak for yourself

THEN Agrippa said unto Paul, Thou art permitted to **speak for thyself**. Then Paul stretched forth the hand, and answered for himself: (Acts 26:1)

Paul was on trial for his life, testifying before the king concerning his witness of Jesus. Paul was allowed to speak on his own behalf, but the expression has come to mean, "Don't talk in the place of others or for others without their consent."

speak into the air

So likewise ye, except ye utter by the tongue words easy to be understood, how shall it be known what is spoken? for ye shall **speak into the air**. (1 Corinthians 14:9)

Speech uttered that is not heard or ineffectual speech is the meaning of this biblical saying. Paul was discussing the subject of speaking in tongues, a controversial issue in his as well as today's church. Paul's point was that the Christian who spoke in tongues without the tongues being a language or having an interpretation would be the same as "speaking into the air."

Speaking in tongues, then, requires a language to be spoken, for that is what "tongue" means in the Bible. Those people speaking in tongues in churches today that aren't uttering real languages are truly "speaking into the air," for nobody knows what they are uttering, and neither does the speaker. God is not impressed and, in fact, condemns utterances of nonsense to him or anyone else.

spy out the land

These *are* the names of the men which Moses sent to **spy out the land**. And Moses called Oshea the son of Nun Jehoshua. (Numbers 13:16)

To check out a place or a situation beforehand is the modern equivalent of this biblical expression still used today. Spies today have sinister reputations, but if we are to do our duty as Moses and his men did, we will also spy out the many lands God puts us into so we can do our best for him.

Sometimes Christians have to do a little undercover work for the Lord. Remember that we are to be "wise as a serpent, and harmless as a dove." You never thought James Bond could help you be a better Christian, did you?

stand in the gap

And I sought for a man among them, that should make up the hedge, and **stand in the gap** before me for the land, that I should not destroy it: but I found none. (Ezekiel 22:30)

Someone who can take up the slack and alleviate a problem that many others can't is said to "stand in the gap." God was looking for such a man to "step up to the plate" as we say, but God could find none that would cause him to appease his intended wrath against Israel.

The heart of the gospel shows itself here, for Jesus is the only man that could actually stand in the gap that separated man and God—the gap of sin and its payment that had to be met. Jesus not only stood in the gap, but he closed it as well, allowing all men to now come to the throne of grace and find "help in time of need."

stand or fall by something

> Who art thou that judgest another man's servant? to his own master he **standeth or falleth**. Yea, he shall be holden up: for God is able to make him stand. (Romans 14:4)

"Do or die," "make it or break it," "stand or fall"—it all means about the same, referring to someone who is putting his reputation behind a matter and putting it on the line.

The Bible is talking about how we answer to our masters (supervisors) and those in authority and no one else. We stand or fall to them just as we do to God. Try calling your boss master; that's who he is according to the Bible.

step between you and death

> And David sware moreover, and said, Thy father certainly knoweth that I have found grace in thine eyes; and he saith, Let not Jonathan know this, lest he be grieved: but truly as the LORD liveth, and as thy soul liveth, there is but **a step between me and death**. (1 Samuel 20:3)

David uttered this exclamation out of fear of King Saul who sought to kill David. David said there was only a "step between me and death," meaning, of course, that death was imminent. David loved King Saul's son Jonathan greatly, "passing the love of women" as it stated in 2 Samuel 1:26.

Some have perverted this love to imply that David and Jonathan were homosexual lovers, but there is no evidence at all for that interpretation. This unfounded accusation is false and only goes to show you what some will do to further their agenda.

The Bible does not condone homosexuality, on the contrary, it condemns it, and not only in the Old Testament, but also in the New. Romans 1:26-7 states: "For this cause God gave them up unto vile affections: for even their women did change the natural use into that which is against nature: And likewise also the men, leaving the natural use of the woman, burned in their lust one toward another; men with men working that which is unseemly, and receiving in themselves that recompense of their error which was meet." With the advent of AIDS, being homosexual or sexually promiscuous today will possibly put "a step between you and death."

stone's throw

And he was withdrawn from them about **a stone's cast**, and kneeled down, and prayed. (Luke 22:41)

Jesus was a short distance or stone's cast away from his disciples just before Judas arrived and gave him the infamous "kiss of death" (see appendix). This is also the incident where Jesus "sweated blood" (see expression "sweat blood").

Despite our modern measurements, we still say something is a "stone's throw" away. We also might say something is a short "piece" away, and the Bible uses that term as well.

straight and narrow

Because **strait** *is* the gate, **and narrow** *is* the way, which leadeth unto life, and few there be that find it. (Matthew 7:14)

To live a virtuous life constitutes walking the straight and narrow path. True Christianity is found only on the narrow way, not the broad way, and "few there be that find it." A few does not mean millions and billions as is claimed for the population of "Christendom."

In the days of Noah, the entire population of the world produced only one righteous man and his family. God said to Noah in Genesis 7:1: "...thee have I seen righteous before me in this generation," meaning the rest of the world was corrupt and would die in the flood since no others were allowed on the boat.

Jesus said the last days would be like the days of Noah as well (Matthew 24:37), so we can expect very few righteous people on the earth. Jesus was not saying that only eight people, like Noah's family, would be saved in the last days. However, there is biblical precedent for whole cities having only one righteous family in it, and Lot in Sodom and Gomorrah was a prime example. God told Abraham he would spare Sodom and Gomorrah if he could find ten righteous men in it, and Abraham could find only Lot and his family, so God destroyed the cities. The world today has many Sodom and Gomorrahs magnified a hundred times more in wickedness. God's got a lot of destroying to do.

straining at gnats

> Ye blind guides, which **strain at a gnat**, and swallow a camel. (Matthew 23:24)

A major characteristic of a Pharisee is his insistence on being what is called a "gnat-strainer"—one who harps on insignificant matters to the neglect of the more serious. "Straining at gnats" is an apt description, for to see a gnat, you do indeed have to strain your eyes, and to see the trivial faults of others requires the same. In the process of being a "fruit inspector," the "camel" is swallowed.

There are those who will use this scripture to preach against all judgment of another's sin, but this is an incorrect application of the teaching. Jesus didn't condemn pointing out another's sin, but only said to remove the "beam" out of your own eye first; then, you will see clearly to remove the "mote" out of your brother's.

stumbling block

> But we preach Christ crucified, unto the Jews a **stumblingblock**, and unto the Greeks foolishness; (1 Corinthians 1:23)

The word "stumbling block" means just what it sounds like—something that causes you to stumble or hinders your progress. Interestingly, one of the names given to Jesus is "stumbling block." In fact, he is the greatest of all stumbling blocks, for in order to get past him, you have to die to your self and sins.

Stumbling causes us to go to our knees, and this is precisely where we need to be in order to make progress in our Christian walk. Forward progress by repeated stumbling may not make a lot of sense, but a baby doesn't learn to walk without it.

such and such

> ¶ Then the king of Syria warred against Israel, and took counsel with his servants, saying, In **such and such** a place *shall be* my camp. (2 Kings 6:8)

When we describe something that we don't want to go in to detail on but is generally understood anyway, we say "so and so" did "such and such." In like manner did the king of Syria as recorded in 2 Kings 6:8 when he was warring with Israel.

suffer fools gladly

> For ye **suffer fools gladly**, seeing ye *yourselves* are wise. (2 Corinthians 11:19)

Having patience with those who are less intelligent than yourself puts you in the group of those who "suffer fools gladly." Paul asked the Corinthian church to bear with him like they did when they suffered other fools gladly. Paul desired to instruct them in some areas they might have considered foolish, warning them that they could be deceived in to accepting "another Jesus" and "another gospel" (verse four).

Just the mention of the name "Jesus," and most assume whom you mean. But which Jesus you're talking about is another story altogether. Are you speaking of the Jesus that some say never did miracles, or are you speaking of the one whom supposedly never claimed he was God? Perhaps you like the loving and kind one who never got angry and would never send anyone to hell (somebody's not reading his Bible). There are many Jesuses, and it is your job to find the real McCoy while "suffering fools gladly" who don't.

sweat blood

And being in an agony he prayed more earnestly: and his **sweat** was as it were great drops of **blood** falling down to the ground. (Luke 22:44)

Working extremely hard or "sweating blood" is found in the account of Jesus praying at the Mount of Olives where it is said he prayed so fervently that his sweat "was as it were great drops of blood." The careful reader will notice that it didn't say he "sweated blood," only that it was "as" blood.

Nonetheless, praying till you sweat in that manner is highly commendable, for the "effectual fervent prayer of a righteous man availeth much (James 5:16).

T

take it easy

And I will say to my soul, Soul, thou hast much goods laid up for many years; **take thine ease**, eat, drink, *and* be merry. (Luke 12:19)

Almost as popular as "goodbye," "take it easy" was essentially the utterance of the rich man in this parable recorded in Luke. The rich man thought he could slack off and "take it easy" because of his accumulated wealth. He also said he wanted to "eat, drink, and be merry," so these phrases have a lot in common.

The Eagles made famous this expression with their song "Take It Easy" in the seventies. This is the philosophy of the world, but God never told anyone to "take it easy." Every time this term is used in scripture, it is in a negative light of slothfulness. David, for example, speaks of the wicked and describes them as "at ease in Zion." From God's perspective, then, you may not want to "take it easy."

take the Lord's name in vain

Thou shalt not take the name of the LORD thy God in vain; for the LORD will not hold him guiltless that **taketh his name in vain**. (Exodus 20:7)

One of the Ten Commandments that is most misunderstood has to be this one from the book of Exodus. Popular misconception states that the expression "taking the Lord's name in vain" means using the name of God haphazardly or in exclamation. That is far from its intended application.

"Taking the Lord's name in vain" means just what it says: actually taking on the name of the Lord for your own benefit without really believing in him in the first place. It is a vain exercise. False religion and its believers are guilty of breaking this commandment on a regular basis.

Why the meaning of this commandment is changed by the unbelievers is quite obvious: the commandment applies directly to them because they pretend to love God by taking on his name but just use him to further their causes.

take under your wing

O Jerusalem, Jerusalem, *thou* that killest the prophets, and stonest them which are sent unto thee, how often would I have gathered thy children together, even as a hen **gathereth** her chickens **under *her* wings**, and ye would not! (Matthew 23:37)

"Taking under your wing" indicates that you like someone enough to take care of him, teach him, and nourish him, if need be. Jesus demonstrates his love for us by comparing what a hen does to its chicks and what he does for his children. David echoed this sentiment by saying in the Psalms, "...hide me under the shadow of thy wings."

take your breath away

Thou hidest thy face, they are troubled: thou **takest away their breath**, they die, and return to their dust. (Psalms 104:29)

Something that is breathtaking is usually a splendid sight or fabulous occurrence. The real breath taker is the Lord himself who actually does, according to the Bible, "take your breath away" when you die. Remember that God in Genesis breathed into Adam and he "became a living soul," so when you die, the Bible says he "takest away their breath." To be breathtaking, then, is not always a good thing. God is breathtaking literally and figuratively, for his looks are breathtaking as well as his actions.

tell it like it is

How hast thou counselled *him that hath* no wisdom? and *how* hast thou plentifully **declared the thing as it is**? (Job 26:3)

Howard Cosell's autobiography *Tell It Like It Is* demonstrated Howard's penchant for not holding anything back in his opinions on sports and its celebrities. When you "tell it like it is," you don't mince words or sugar-coat anything, and that's the way God likes it.

God asked Job if he was telling it like it is in reference to telling others about the gospel. True Christians should not hesitate in telling it like it is, for the true gospel will always offend. If it doesn't, then you're watering it down with niceties.

Worrying about offending others should cause you to examine yourself to see whether you "be in the faith." Jesus offended people everywhere he went, and as the world itself acknowledges, "The truth hurts."

tender mercies (leave to one's)

Remember, O LORD, thy **tender mercies** and thy lovingkindnesses; for they *have been* ever of old. (Psalm 25:6)

To leave someone to another's tender mercies is to leave that person in the care of another who isn't so appealing for one reason or another. "Tender mercies" takes on a different meaning in scripture, signifying God's literal mercy on us.

Tender Mercies shows up as the title of a movie released in the last few years, but it doesn't have much to do with God's mercy. Movie producers, book writers, and others find it more and more necessary to use the Bible as a source for their titles, having used thousands of biblical phrases over the years (see appendices of movie and song titles using biblical expressions).

their name is legion

And he asked him, What *is* thy name?   And he answered, saying, **My name *is* Legion**: for we are many. (Mark 5:9)

You hear this phrase used often to denote those whose accomplishments are legendary or famous. "Legion" means to be numerous as it does also in the Bible. In this account, Jesus cast out devils who called themselves "Legion" and sent them into a herd of swine.

Does this mean that animals can be possessed? They were in this instance, and Satan most certainly uses animals for his purposes. "Beware of dogs" takes on new significance, now doesn't it?

there but for the grace of God go I

But by the grace of God I am what I am: and his grace which *was bestowed* upon me was not in vain; but I laboured more abundantly than they all: yet not I, but the grace of God which was with me.   (1 Corinthians 15:10)

Paul recounted his past by stating he persecuted the church of God heavily before his conversion. The expression "by the grace of God" is used quite often by those who have had some particular downfall in their lives and were helped by God in their time of need.

His grace is truly amazing, for the only real difference between a sinner and a saint is God's grace. Every saint can say, "There but for the grace of God go I" when he speaks of what might have happened to him had he followed the crowds and not the way of God. We should never reach the point of pride where we can't acknowledge that God surely did, as the hymn says, "save a wretch like us."

there's a time for everything

TO every *thing there is* a season, and **a time to every purpose** under the heaven: (Ecclesiastes 3:1)

Isn't it strange that you hear people say, "There's a time for everything," yet they don't realize where that statement originates. King Solomon penned this in Ecclesiastes long before the group the Birds sang about it. Solomon goes in detail on the appropriate times for many things, saying there is a "time to love, and a time to hate," a "time to kill, and a time to heal."

Hating and killing ought to go over real well with the "I don't hate anyone or kill anything" crowd. Anyone thinking logically should realize that in order to be consistent, it is impossible to love everybody or everything. True love hates evil, and it hates everything that destroys true love. You can't love the truth and love a lie at the same time. They are mutually exclusive and diametrically opposed.

thorn in my side

And lest I should be exalted above measure through the abundance of the revelations, there was given to me **a thorn in the flesh**, the messenger of Satan to buffet me, lest I should be exalted above measure. (2 Corinthians 12:7)

Each of us usually has something we can point to as a "thorn in our side," a commonly spoken phrase meaning a constant irritation that is mental or physical. The apostle Paul mentioned that God gave him a "thorn" in order for Paul not to be "exalted above measure," or, in other words, to humble him.

Paul's thorn was a big one, a "messenger of Satan" to "buffet" him. Who this "messenger of Satan" was the scriptures do not say. Many of us should be thankful that our thorns aren't so sharp. The prettiest rose didn't grow without thorns.

through a glass darkly

For now we see **through a glass, darkly**; but then face to face: now I know in part, but then shall I know even as also I am known. (1 Corinthians 13:12)

The biblical expression "through a glass darkly" describes how we don't see the spiritual world very clearly at present. When we are changed and enter into heaven, then we will "know even also as I am known," said Paul.

The Bible does say that "Eye hath not seen, nor ear heard, neither have entered into the heart of man, the things which God hath prepared for them that love him" (1 Corinthians 2:9).

Notice that it said that eyes haven't seen the things of heaven. All these people on their deathbeds who say they went to heaven and saw all these marvelous things and came back to life can't be true according to the Bible, for God won't let them see these things as of yet. God gives us his own preview of the coming attractions in written form.

toss and turn

He will surely violently **turn and toss** thee *like* a ball into a large country: there shalt thou die, and there the chariots of thy glory *shall be* the shame of thy lord's house. (Isaiah 22:18)

After a bad night's sleep, we might say that we "tossed and turned." The Bible's use of this phrase doesn't involve a bad night's sleep. The Lord was pronouncing judgment on a certain Shebna, a treasurer of the Persians, for his invasion of Israel. God said he would "turn and toss" him like a ball. Who says God doesn't play ball? He plays it with people.

turn the other cheek

But I say unto you, That ye resist not evil: but whosoever shall smite thee on thy right **cheek, turn to him the other also**. (Matthew 5:39)

When's the last time someone hit you in the face, and you didn't want to hit him back but "turned the other cheek"? It's not the easiest of things to do, but it is a commandment of the Lord who did this very thing when he was struck on the face several times by his enemies.

We apply this expression to non-violent matters also, telling others to "turn the other cheek" and not seek revenge when someone does something to them that upsets them. Instead of hitting them back, just ask God to "break their teeth in their mouth" like David did, the man after God's own heart. The Lord likes to fight his own battles, and he can do the job that needs to be done.

twinkling of an eye

> In a moment, **in the twinkling of an eye**, at the last trump: for the trumpet shall sound, and the dead shall be raised incorruptible, and we shall be changed, (1 Corinthians 15:52)

Also known as "in the blink of an eye," this phrase is used to denote things happening in an instant, like the actual blink of an eye. In this passage, God talks of changing our bodies "in the twinkling of an eye" at the rapture of the saints. "People just don't disappear" some say when looking for someone. The Bible would respectfully disagree. We most certainly do disappear, and disappearing is the one thing a Christian should be looking forward to the most. David Copperfield would be proud.

two-edged sword (double-edged)

> For the word of God *is* quick, and powerful, and sharper than any **two-edged sword**, piercing even to the dividing asunder of soul and spirit, and of the joints and marrow, and *is* a discerner of the thoughts and intents of the heart. (Hebrews 4:12)

A "double-edged sword" is anything that produces both good and bad effects simultaneously. There could be no better example of a double-edged sword than the Bible, for it cuts to the heart like a sword and will either save your soul and change your heart or condemn your soul and harden your heart.

One reason that the Bible is so avoided by some is that it reveals, as it says, our own "thoughts and intents" to us. It reaches into the very recesses of our soul and makes us face our real selves, and that's not a pretty sight.

Like any two-edged sword, the Bible is very dangerous if mishandled, i.e., misinterpreted. It will cut you in to pieces if you're not careful. Just like God himself, the Bible kills and makes alive. Whether we want it to kill us or make us alive is our choice.

two heads are better than one

¶ **Two _are_ better than one**; because they have a good reward for their labour. (Ecclesiastes 4:9)

Anybody working together on project knows that it's sometimes better to have the opinion of others to help you make a decision than by yourself, and that is the meaning of this expression.

The Bible reference is to marriage, and how "two heads are better than one" when it comes to coping together with life's problems.

U

under the sun

> SO I returned, and considered all the oppressions that are done **under the sun**: and behold the tears of *such as were* oppressed, and they had no comforter; and on the side of their oppressors *there was* power; but they had no comforter. (Ecclesiastes 4:1)

Instead of saying "all" of something, we might say "everything under the sun" because that would include just about anything.

Jesus, interestingly enough, is called the "Sun of Righteousness" in Malachi 4:2 (that's "*Sun*" with a "*u*"). Besides their same name, he and the sun have a lot in common, and that is no coincidence. Both have risen in the East, both give light and life, and both are a "consuming fire" that could kill us in an instant if we approached too close. There are many more parallels in nature and in the heavens, for "The heavens declare the glory of God" as it says in Psalm 19.

V

voice in the wilderness

¶ The **voice** of him that crieth **in the wilderness**, Prepare ye the way of the LORD, make straight in the desert a highway for our God. (Isaiah 40:3)

"A voice in the wilderness" is anyone that is perceived as a lone protester with very little support. John the Baptist was the original voice in the wilderness who cried out about the coming Messiah and how he would change the hearts of the children.

Every prophet of God has been a voice in the wilderness, and every Christian is like one also because he is surrounded by the ungodly lifestyle of a wicked nation. The true voice of God is not heard on every street corner or on every religious broadcast. Instead, it is heard in the wilderness by the few who dare cry out.

W-Z

wages of sin

> For **the wages of sin** *is* death: but the gift of God *is* eternal life through Jesus Christ our Lord. (Romans 6:23)

Everything has its price, and sin is no exception. It just so happens that the "wages of sin," i.e., the consequence or price of sin, is the most expensive you will ever encounter—eternal damnation in a burning hell. Sin exacts heavy wages of which we can never fully repay, and no amount of money we offer can pay its debts. Jesus, however, paid the price that was accepted by God, for the price was the blood of God himself in the person of Jesus Christ.

Everyone must make the decision of whether his sins are worth the price of eternal damnation. If they are worth damnation to an individual, then he will meet his debts on a never-ending long-term payment plan in hell. God would like to re-finance your spiritual mortgage if need be.

wash your hands of something

> ¶ When Pilate saw that he could prevail nothing, but *that* rather a tumult was made, he took water, and **washed *his* hands** before the multitude, saying, I am innocent of the blood of this just person: see ye *to it*. (Matthew 27:24)

"Washing your hands" of a matter says that you are no longer taking any responsibility for a situation and are pronouncing yourself clear of any accountability to it. Pilate refused to take part in the condemning of Jesus to the cross, so he gave it over to the multitudes who crucified him anyway.

Refusing to make a choice about Jesus occurs on the individual level as well, but washing your hands of the Lord doesn't exonerate you. Jesus said, "He that is not with me is against me," so that rules out all the agnostics out there who claim they just don't know enough to make a decision. Jesus says they do, but that they just refuse to do so.

weighed in the balance (weighed and wanting)

TEKEL; Thou art **weighed in the balances**, and art found wanting. (Daniel 5:27)

The "writing on the wall" incident (see expression "writing on the wall") where God's hand appeared and wrote on a wall during a big party that King Belshazzar threw is the context of the biblical expression "weighed and wanting." The message that God wrote on the wall translated to include the words of this phrase "weighed in the balance."

Today, this expression speaks of the deficiencies of an individual and how they relate to the matter at hand. Those of you who think God will actually weigh your deeds will all come up "weighed and wanting" and thereby be deficient of God's requirements. None of your deeds are considered good without belief in him, no matter how many so-called good deeds you do.

We must all remember that God's scale includes not only actions, but also speech and even our thoughts. That's definitely not a scale that is tipped in our favor.

weaker vessel

Likewise, ye husbands, dwell with *them* according to knowledge, giving honour unto the wife, as unto the **weaker vessel**, and as being heirs together of the grace of life; that your prayers be not hindered. (1 Peter 3:7)

As you might expect, this is not a particularly popular expression with the feminist movement today. Though women are the weaker vessel, this does not mean that women are somehow less of a person than a man; it's just that they have different roles to fulfill.

Yes, women are for the most part physically weaker; just compare any of them to men in any sport or physical contest. It's usually no contest. If women really do want total equality, then they should not separate themselves in to women's sports.

The man is also considered stronger spiritually, for he is the "head of the house" (see "man of the house") and in charge of spiritual leadership primarily because he is stronger. The serpent sought to tempt Eve, the weak link. The scriptures say that Eve, not Adam, was deceived.

Though the woman is the weaker vessel, any man can tell you that she has certain strengths that can't be equaled by man. The ironic thing is that she has the ability to make man a weaker vessel and does so on a regular basis.

went to do your business

> And it came to pass about this time, that *Joseph* **went** into the house **to do his business**; and *there was* none of the men of the house there within. (Genesis 39:11)

It's really strange what pops up in the Bible, isn't it? You probably wouldn't expect this phrase to be there, but it is. Yes, "going to do your business" does mean going to the bathroom, in the Bible as well as in modern use. Joseph, the son of Isaac, has the distinction of being one of the few persons in scriptures who is said to have gone to the bathroom.

There is another reference to this activity, and the Bible has another special term for it—"covering your feet." In Judges 3:24, Ehud is doing his business and "covering his feet" in his summer chamber. If you think about it, "covering your feet" is an appropriate description, for that is exactly what we do with our pants when we sit down in the bathroom. Who says God doesn't have humor? He does, but it's more of the dry kind mixed with stinging sarcasm.

what have we here?

> Now therefore, **what have I here**, saith the LORD, that my people is taken away for nought? they that rule over them make them to howl, saith the LORD; and my name continually every day *is* blasphemed. (Isaiah 52:5)

You often hear this rhetorical question asked when someone discovers something of significance or surprise. God himself used it when musing over Israel's captivity by another nation. Of course, it wasn't a surprise to God, but it showed some of the personality of God through his use of rhetorical language.

wheels within wheels

> The appearance of the wheels and their work *was* like unto the colour of a beryl: and they four had one likeness: and their appearance and their work *was* as it were a **wheel in the middle of a wheel**. (Ezekiel 1:16)

"Wheels within wheels" is a picturesque illustration of the complexity of a situation that is not readily apparent to those on the outside. Literally speaking, "wheels within wheels" depicts the operations of modern clocks, transmissions, and other such things.

Ezekiel's visions of living creatures appeared to him as "wheels within wheels," not only for what they looked like, but also how they operated together.

It's also an excellent analogy of the operations of God in our lives, for he does things for a multitude of reasons and purposes that we don't always understand, but we eventually see that he runs his show like a well-oiled machine.

when the spirit moves you

And the **Spirit of the Lord began to move him** at times in the camp of Dan between Zorah and Eshtaol. (Judges 13:25)

Telling people to act "whenever the spirit moves you" indicates that you are permitting them to do things whenever they feel like it. The Bible doesn't use this cliché figuratively, but applies it to Samuel and how the Spirit of God really did begin to move him as a child.

When the world speaks of the "spirit moving you," ask them to what spirit are they referring, for there are many spirits out there, and God is only one of them.

wise in your own eyes

For I would not, brethren, that ye should be ignorant of this mystery, lest ye should be **wise in your own conceits**; that blindness in part is happened to Israel, until the fulness of the Gentiles be come in. (Romans 11:25)

Paul was concerned that some of his church members might be "wise in their own eyes," meaning that they were wise only to themselves and not in the minds of others. Paul called it "wise in your own conceits," but it is the same idea.

You don't hear that word "*conceit*" used much anymore. It has been replaced with "*self-esteem*," making arrogance seem respectable. The Bible does talk about esteem, but not self-esteem. It says we should esteem others higher than ourselves; it also says to esteem the words of his mouth more than our own food (Job). It doesn't say how we should love ourselves and how important our "self" is—that is all psychological mumbo-jumbo, and the Bible condemns it. Man has no trouble loving himself. That's actually part of the problem.

with a vengeance

Say to them *that are* of a fearful heart, Be strong, fear not: behold, your God will come **_with_ vengeance**, *even* God *with* a recompence; he will come and save you. (Isaiah 35:4)

Acting with a vengeance denotes actions that are hard, swift, sure, and determined. Another famous biblical quote involving vengeance has God saying, "Vengeance is mine, I will repay."

God certainly will repay the wicked and that dreadfully so. When Jesus returns, his wrath is so great on the unbeliever that the book of Isaiah says Jesus' garments are soaked with their blood: "Wherefore *art thou* red in thine apparel, and thy garments like him that treadeth in the winefat? I have trodden the winepress alone; and of the people *there was* none with me: for I will tread them in mine anger, and trample them in my fury; and their blood shall be sprinkled upon my garments, and I will stain all my raiment" (Isaiah 63:2-3).

Surprisingly, this ghastly account is what is being referred to in the famous "Battle Hymn of the Republic" song: "He is trampling out the vintage where the grapes of wrath are strewn; ...his truth is marching on." Most of us sing this without realizing that we're singing about God systematically wiping out the wicked at his return. Go on singing and don't feel bad. The Bible says the righteous should rejoice at the destruction of the wicked (see Revelation 18:20).

with you in spirit

For though I be absent in the flesh, yet am I **with you in the spirit**, joying and beholding your order, and the steadfastness of your faith in Christ. (Colossians 2:5)

To be with someone "in spirit" is to be with him in your thoughts. Paul was talking how he was with his church in the spirit.

When a Christian says he is "with you in spirit," he can literally mean it, for each Christian has the same spirit of God in him. Since all believers are in the Holy Spirit which is omnipresent, they are with each other in spirit as well.

woe is me!

> **Woe is me**, that I sojourn in Mesech, *that* I dwell in the tents of Kedar! (Psalms 120:5)

David lamented of his troubles and gloom by exclaiming the adage "Woe is me," but he knew that his woes were nothing compared to the woes that await the wicked. Jesus throughout the gospels proclaimed "Woe unto you" when speaking unto the wicked and the Pharisees. "Woe unto you," of course, means calamity and doom is coming your way.

If anyone should proclaim, "Woe is me," it is the wicked. In Revelation 12:12, God speaks of their doom: "Therefore rejoice, *ye* heavens, and ye that dwell in them. Woe to the inhabiters of the earth and of the sea! for the devil is come down unto you, having great wrath, because he knoweth that he hath but a short time."

This passage refers to the antichrist, Satan incarnate, who will bring a false peace to the earth and cause many to receive the mark of the beast, one of the many woes that await the unsaved.

wolf in sheep's clothing

> ¶ Beware of false prophets, which come to you **in sheep's clothing**, but inwardly they are ravening **wolves**. (Matthew 7:15)

Jesus warned his followers of "wolves in sheep's clothing" who were false prophets pretending to be ministers of the gospel. You know the type; they wear nice "sheep's clothing" (wool suits) and talk about God to deceive the masses for their money.

A child of God should be able to recognize these charlatans because Jesus said, "My sheep hear my voice, and I know them, and they follow me" (John 10:27). Anyone can recognize a wolf; it's the wolf in sheep's clothing that you need to be discerning.

won't lift a finger

> For they bind heavy burdens and grievous to be borne, and lay *them* on men's shoulders; but they *themselves* **will not move them with one of their fingers**. (Matthew 23:4)

This was another in a long line of railing accusations against the Pharisees. Jesus said they wouldn't "move...one of their fingers" to help others. Pharisees love to talk about their concern for the unfortunate, but when it comes down to actually doing something, that spirit of kindness somehow disappears or is masqueraded behind an act of kindness for some devious purpose.

word is gone out

> I have sworn by myself, **the word is gone out** of my mouth *in* righteousness, and shall not return, That unto me every knee shall bow, every tongue shall swear. (Isaiah 45:23)

When we say "the word has gone out," we refer to a matter being made known to the masses. If only the world could have done as good a job as God in "getting the word out," it would have accomplished a huge feat. The word of God has literally gone out to all the world, and God didn't need a slick marketing campaign to get it done.

The God of the Old Testament that said every knee would bow to him is the same God in the New Testament (Phillipians 2:10) whom every knee would also bow to: "That at the name of Jesus every knee should bow, of *things* in heaven, and *things* in earth, and *things* under the earth;" We're not bowing down to two separate beings.

writing on the wall

¶ In the same hour came forth fingers of a man's hand, and **wrote** over against the candlestick **upon the plaister of the wall** of the king's palace: and the king saw the part of the hand that wrote. (Daniel 5:5)

Can't you just see the big party King Belshazzar was throwing? Everyone was getting drunk and living it up. All of the sudden, a hand appears out of nowhere and starts writing on the wall. It was a message to the king that his life had been judged and was found quite lacking. The king was so scared that the Bible says his knees started shaking.

"Writing on the wall" refers to the inevitable, unfortunate circumstances that await an individual. When the individual realizes what's getting ready to occur, he sees "the writing on the wall." If you don't see "the writing on the wall," you better check your spiritual barometer.

written in stone

But if the ministration of death, **written** *and* engraven **in stones**, was glorious, so that the children of Israel could not steadfastly behold the face of Moses for the glory of his countenance; which *glory* was to be done away: How shall not the ministration of the spirit be rather glorious? (2 Corinthians 3:7-8)

If it's not written in stone, the plans or directives aren't finalized, or they can be altered easily if they are. The world loves to alter and amend its written codes—just look at our Constitution and laws.

When God gave us the Ten Commandments written in stone, he was showing us the permanency of the word of God and its need for no alterations whatsoever. Our Bibles should be treated as if every page were written in stone, for some of them actually were!

you're the man!

And Nathan said to David, **Thou _art_ the man**. Thus saith the Lord God of Israel, I annointed thee king over Israel, and I delivered thee out of the hand of Saul; (2 Samuel 12:7)

Nathan the prophet had just gotten through telling David a parable of a rich man and a poor man, the poor man having nothing but a ewe lamb. A traveler had come and taken the poor man's lamb, and this story greatly angered David. Nathan then told David that David was "the man," that traveler in the story.

This story was told in reference to David's sin of getting his men to put Uriah the Hittite in a battle to kill Uriah and then for David to get his wife Bath-sheba. If you remember the famous story, David had just seen Bath-sheba bathing on a rooftop and lusted after her.

Though the phrase "you are the man" indicates someone who thinks another is a highly admirable person, in the Bible, it was a finger-pointing accusation towards an adulterous murderer.

Afterword

According to Genesis 2:19, when Adam was created, he was already endued with the gift of language because he had the ability to give names to all the animals. Because Adam was the only human on the planet (talk about lonely!), he did not learn language from anyone but God. Thus, man did not invent language according to the Bible. God gave man a language to speak and the ability to learn it. From Adam through his descendants we all learned to communicate.

Since all the world spoke only one language until the Tower of Babel incident, we can also surmise that the characteristics of this one language were carried over into the other languages that God also created, for if you remember, man did not invent other languages either, but God "did there confound the language of all the earth" (Genesis 11:9).

The existence of all the world's languages is one of the greatest proofs of the existence of God as mentioned earlier in this work. The fact that God was and still is very involved in our use and style of language has been a theme promulgated throughout this work.

As he did with Adam, God is still teaching us language today through the Bible's numerous quaint and colorful expressions. Let us rejoice as King David did when he said the following: "Princes have persecuted me without a cause: but my heart standeth in awe of thy word. I rejoice at thy word, as one that findeth great spoil" (Psalm 119:161-2). The Bible is an inexhaustible treasure that most of the world has yet to fully discover.

Bibliography

Ammer, Christine. *Have a Nice Day—No Problem!* New York: Penguin Books USA Inc., 1992.

Castell, Ron, ed. *Blockbuster Video Guide to Movies and Videos 1996.* New York: Dell Publishing, 1995.

Claiborne, Robert. *Loose Cannons and Red Herrings: A Book of Lost Metaphors.* New York: W.W. Norton Company, 1988.

Craig, Doris. *Catch Phrases, Cliches, and Idioms.* Jefferson, North Carolina: McFarland and Company, Inc., 1990.

Dictionary of Phrase and Fable. New Lanark, Scotland: Brockhampton Press, 1995.

Doege, Danny C. *Why We Say, What We Say!* No Publisher, 1994.

Ehrlich, Eugene, and David H. Scott. *Mene, Mene, Tekel.* New York: HarperCollins Publishers, 1990.

Evans, Ivor H., ed. *Brewer's Dictionary of Phrase and Fable.* 14 ed. NewYork: Harper and Row Publishers, 1989.

Kirkpatrick, E.M. and C.M. Schwarz editors. *The Wordsworth Dictionary of Idioms.* Ware, Hertfordshire: Wordsworth Editions Ltd., 1993.

Lass, Abraham H., David Kiremedjran, and Ruth M. Goldstein. *The Dictionary of Classical, Biblical and Literary Allusions.* New York: Ballantine Books, 1987.

Macrone, Michael. *Brush Up Your Bible!* New York: HarperCollins Publishers, 1993.

Maltin, Leonard, ed. *TV Movies and Video Guide 1989 Edition.* New York: NAL Penguin INC., 1988.

Manser, Martin H. ed. *I Never Knew That Was in the Bible.* Nashville: Thomas Nelson Publishers, 1999.

McNeil, Alex. *Total Television.* 3rd rev. ed. New York: Viking Penguin, 1991.

Partridge, Eric. *A Dictionary of Cliches with an Introductory Essay.* 5th ed. New York: Routledge and Kegan Ltd., 1978.

Rogers, James. *The Dictionary of Cliches*. New York: Ballantine Books, 1985.

Rosenthal, Peggy and George Dardess. *Every Cliché in the Book*. New York: William Morrow and Company, Inc., 1987.

Simpson, J.A., ed. *The Concise Oxford Dictionary of Proverbs*. New York: Oxford University Press, 1982.

Smyth, Alice Mary et al. *The Oxford Dictionary of Quotations*. 2nd ed. New York: Oxford University Press, 1955.

Terrace, Vincent. *The Complete Encyclopedia of Television Programs 1947-1979*. 2nd ed. rev. 2 vols. New York: A.S. Barnes and Company, Inc., 1979.

Wright, Larry. *Happy as a Clam and 9,999 Other Similes*. New York: Prentice Hall General Reference, 1994.

Appendix A
Once Popular Biblical Expressions Used Less Frequently Today

abomination of desolation
> (a detestable thing)

> When ye therefore shall see **the abomination of desolation**, spoken of by Daniel the prophet, stand in the holy place, (whoso readeth, let him understand:) (Matthew 24:16)

Abraham's bosom
> (paradise, heaven, or bliss)

> And it came to pass, that the beggar died, and was carried by the angels into **Abraham's bosom**: the rich man also died, and was buried; (Luke 16:22)

Ancient of Days
> (Another name for Jesus)

> ¶ I beheld till the thrones were cast down, and **the Ancient of days** did sit, whose garment *was* white as snow, and the hair of his head like the pure wool: his throne *was like* the fiery flame, *and* his wheels *as* burning fire. (Daniel 7:9)

answer a fool according to his foolishness
> (give a foolish answer to a fool)

> **Answer a fool according to his folly**, lest he be wise in his own conceit. (Proverbs 26:5)

as one man
> (people acting in unison)

¶ And all the people arose **as one man**, saying, We will not any *of us* go to his tent, neither will we any *of us* turn into his house. (Judges 20:8)

ask for bread and receive a stone
(to get much less than requested)

Or what man is there of you, whom if his son **ask bread, will he give him a stone**? (Matthew 7:9)

balm in Gilead
(something soothing; relief)

Is there no **balm in Gilead**; *is there* no physician there? why then is not the health of the daughter of my people recovered? (Jeremiah 8:22)

be of good cheer
(happy and content)

These things have I spoken unto you, that in me ye might have peace. In the world ye shall have tribulation: but **be of good cheer**; I have overcome the world. (John 16:33)

bear false witness
(lie or deceive)

He saith unto him, Which? Jesus said, Thou shalt do no murder, Thou shalt not commit adultery, Thou shalt not steal, Thou shalt not **bear false witness**, (Matthew 19:18)

beard the lion
(confront a dangerous situation)

And I went out after him, and smote him, and delivered *it* out of his mouth: and when he arose against me, I **caught *him* by his beard**, and smote him, and slew him. (1 Samuel 17:35)

before the flood
(ancient times; a long time ago)

And Joshua said unto all the people, Thus saith the LORD God of Israel, Your fathers dwelt on **the other side of the flood** in old time, *even* Terah, the father of Abraham, and the father of Nachor: and they served other gods. (Joshua 24:2)

bound hand and foot
(tied up at the hands and feet)

And he that was dead came forth, **bound hand and foot** with graveclothes and his face was bound about with a napkin. Jesus saith unto them, Loose him, and let him go. (John 11:44)

broken reed
(an unreliable person or thing)

Lo, thou trustest in the staff of this **broken reed**, on Egypt; whereon if a man lean, it will go into his hand, and pierce it: so *is* Pharaoh king of Egypt to all that trust in him. (Isaiah 36:6)

burnt offering
(an over cooked meal)

¶ And Noah builded an altar unto the LORD; and took of every clean beast, and of every clean fowl, and offered **burnt offerings** on the altar. (Genesis 8:20)

camel through the eye of a needle
(an obvious impossibility)

And again I say unto you, It is easier for **a camel to go through the eye of a needle**, than for a rich man to enter into the kingdom of God. (Matthew 19:24)

cast in your lot with
(put your money in the kitty)

Cast in thy lot among us; let us all have one purse: (Proverbs 1:14)

cast into outer darkness
(banished, shut out)

But the children of the kingdom shall be **cast out into outer darkness**: there shall be weeping and gnashing of teeth. (Matthew 8:12)

cast out devils
(to change a person's evil ways)

Many will say to me in that day, Lord, Lord, have we not prophesied in thy name? and in thy name have **cast out devils**? and in thy name done many wonderful works? (Matthew 7:22)

cast pearls before swine
(offering to others who don't appreciate it)

¶ Give not that which is holy unto the dogs, neither **cast ye your pearls before swine**, lest they trample them under their feet, and turn again and rend you. (Matthew 7:6)

cast your bread upon the waters
(to take a chance through investment)

CAST thy bread upon the waters: for thou shalt find It after many days. (Ecclesiastes 11:1)

chew the cud
> (to contemplate, consider)

> Nevertheless these shall ye not eat of them that **chew the cud**, or of them that divide the hoof: *as* the camel, because he cheweth the cud, but divideth not the hoof; he *is* unclean unto you. (Leviticus 11:4)

child of the devil
> (an evil person)

> And said, O full of all subtilty and all mischief, thou **child of the devil**, thou enemy of all righteousness, wilt thou not cease to pervert the right ways of the Lord? (Acts 13:10)

children of this world
> (the unsaved masses; heathen)

> And the lord commended the unjust steward, because he had done wisely: for **the children of this world** are in their generation wiser than the children of light. (Luke 16:8)

citizen of no mean city
> (a resident of a well-known city)

> But Paul said, I am a man *which am* a Jew of Tarsus, *a city* in Cilicia, **a citizen of no mean city**: and, I beseech thee, suffer me to speak unto the people. (Acts 21:39)

cloud no bigger than a man's hand
> (an omen or warning)

> And it came to pass at the seventh time, that he said, Behold, there ariseth **a little cloud** out of the sea, **like a man's hand**. And he said, Go up, say unto Ahab,

Prepare *thy chariot*, and get thee down, that the rain stop thee not. (1 Kings 18:44)

cloud of witnesses
(a multitude of eyewitnesses)

WHEREFORE seeing we also are compassed about with so great **a cloud of witnesses**, let us lay aside every weight, and the sin which doth so easily beset *us*, and let us run with patience the race that is set before us, (Hebrews 12:1)

cover a multitude of sins
(inclusive of many different items or ideas)

And above all things have fervent charity among your-selves: for charity shall **cover the multitude of sins**. (1 Peter 4:8)

crown of glory
(an outstanding accomplishment)

And when the chief Shepherd shall appear, ye shall receive **a crown of glory** that fadeth not away. (1 Peter 5:4)

cup runneth over, one's
(to have an abundance)

Thou preparest a table before me in the presence of mine enemies: thou annointest my head with oil; **my cup runneth over**. (Psalm 23:5)

daily bread
(one's physical needs)

Give us this day our **daily bread**. (Matthew 6:11)

darken counsel

(cloud the issue or prevent dialogue)

Who *is* this **darkeneth counsel** by words without knowledge? (Job 38:2)

deaf as an adder
(not good of hearing)

Their poison is like the poison of a serpent: they are **like the deaf adder** that stoppeth her ear; (Psalm 58:4)

divide the spoils
(split up goods amongst others)

Thou hast multiplied the nation, *and* not increased the joy: they joy before thee according to the joy in harvest, *and* as *men* rejoice when they **divide the spoil**. (Isaiah 9:3)

draw a bow at a venture
(to take a chance at something)

And a *certain* man **drew a bow at a venture**, and smote the king of Israel between the joints of the harness: therefore he said to his chariot man, Turn thine hand, that thou mayest carry me out of the host; for I am wounded. (2 Chronicles 18:33)

enemy is at the gate
(trouble is near)

As arrows *are* in the hand of a mighty man; so *are* children of the youth. Happy *is* the man that hath his quiver full of them: they shall not be ashamed, but they shall speak with **the enemies in the gate**. (Psalm 127:5)

escape the bear and fall to the lion

(to go from bad to worse)

As if a man did **flee from a lion, and a bear met him**; or went into the house, and leaned his hand on the wall, and a serpent bit him. (Amos 5:19)

ewe lamb
(what one treasures the most)

But the poor *man* had nothing, save one little **ewe lamb**, which he had bought and nourished up: and it grew up together with him, and with his children; it did eat of his own meat, and drank of his own cup, and lay in his bosom, and was unto him as a daughter. (2 Samuel 12:3)

fall of a sparrow
(the importance of little things)

Are not two **sparrows** sold for a farthing? and one of them shall not **fall** on the ground without your Father. (Matthew 10:29)

fall on stony ground
(an idea that does not win acceptance or approval)

And some **fell on stony ground**, where it had not much earth; and immediately it sprang up, because it had no depth of earth: (Mark 4:5)

fallen angel
(someone who has morally degenerated)

How art thou **fallen from heaven, O Lucifer**, son of the morning! *how* art thou cut down to the ground, which didst weaken the nations! (Isaiah 14:12)

fear and trembling

(sarcastic apprehension or fright)

And his inward affection is more abundant toward you, whilst he remembereth the obedience of you all, how with **fear and trembling** ye received him. (2 Corinthians 7:15)

fearfully and wonderfully made
(anything of complex design)

I will praise thee; for I am **fearfully *and* wonderfully made**: marvellous *are* thy works; and *that* my soul knoweth right well. (Psalm 139:14)

finger of God
(recognize God's work in a matter)

Then the magicians said unto Pharaoh, This *is* **the finger of God**: and Pharaoh's heart was hardened, and he hearkened not unto them; as the LORD had said. (Exodus 8:19)

flesh-pots of Egypt
(creature comforts that are missed)

And the children of Israel said unto them, Would to God we had died by the hand of the LORD in the land **of Egypt**, when we sat **by the flesh pots**, *and* when we did eat bread to the full; for ye have brought us forth into this wilderness, to kill this whole assembly with hunger. (Exodus 16:3)

fruit of my labor
(to see the results of one's work)

But if I live in the flesh, this *is* the **fruit of my labour**: yet what I shall choose I wot not. (Phillipians 1:22)

fullness of time

(the appointed or right time)

But when **the fulness of the time** was come, God sent forth his Son, made of a woman, made under the law, (Galatians 4:4)

gall and wormwood
(a bitter experience to endure)

Remembering mine affliction and my misery, the **wormwood and the gall**. (Lamentations 3:19)

gathered to your fathers
(to die)

And also all that generation were **gathered unto their fathers**: and there arose another generation after them, which knew not the LORD, nor yet the works which he had done for Israel. (Judges 2:10)

gift of tongues
(multilingual)

And God hath set some in the church, first apostles, secondarily prophets, thirdly teachers, after that miracles, then gifts of healings, helps, governments, **diversities of tongues**. (1 Corinthians 12:28)

gird up your loins
(to get ready for strenuous work or action)

AND Elisha the prophet called one of the children of the prophets, and said unto him, **Gird up thy loins**, and take this box of oil in thine hand, and go to Ramoth-gilead: (2 Kings 9:1)

God and Mammon
(the choice between serving God and riches)

¶ No man can serve two masters: for either he will hate the one, and love the other; or else he will hold to the one, and despise the other. Ye cannot serve **God and mammon**. (Matthew 6:24)

good men and true
(reliable, honest people)

¶ And, behold, *there was* a man named Joseph, a counsellor; *and he was* **a good man, and a just**: (Luke 23:50)

greater love hath no man
(the greatest sacrifice you can make for another)

Greater love hath no man than this, that a man lay down his life for his friends. (John 15:13)

grind the face of someone
(to govern harshly)

What mean ye *that* ye beat my people to pieces, and **grind the faces of the poor**? saith the Lord God of hosts. (Isaiah 3:15)

hand against every man, one's
(the acts of criminals and rebels)

And he will be a wild man; his **hand *will be* against every man**, and every man's hand against him; and he shall dwell in the presence of his brethren. (Genesis 16:12)

hand has lost its cunning, one's
(skills are deteriorating)

If I forget thee, O Jerusalem, let my right **hand forget *her cunning***. (Psalm 137:5)

have your feet on another's neck
(domination over someone)

And it came to pass, when they brought out those kings unto Joshua, that Joshua called for all the men of Israel, and said unto the captains of the men of war which went with him, Come near, put your feet upon the necks of these kings. And they came near, and **put their feet upon the necks of them**. (Joshua 10:24)

heap coals of fire on one's head
(doing good to your enemies)

For thou shalt **heap coals of fire upon his head**, and the LORD shall reward thee. (Proverbs 25:22)

heart of stone
(an unemotional individual)

A new heart also will I give you, and a new spirit will I put within you: and I will take away the **stony heart** out of your flesh, and I will give you an heart of flesh. (Ezekiel 36:26)

hewers of wood and drawers of water
(lowest level workers)

And the princes said unto them, Let them live; but let them be **hewers of wood and drawers of water** unto all the congregation; as the princes had promised them. (Joshua 9:21)

hide your light under a bushel
(conceal one's abilities out of modesty)

Neither do men **light** a candle, and **put it under a bushel**, but on a candlestick; and it giveth light unto all that are in the house. (Matthew 5:15)

hope deferred
(when one's hopes and dreams are delayed)

Hope deferred maketh the heart sick: but *when* the desire cometh, *it is* a tree of life. (Proverbs 13:12)

howling wilderness
(a scary place or situation)

He found him in a desert land, and in the waste **howling wilderness**; he led him about, he instructed him, he kept him as the apple of his eye. (Deut. 32:10)

inner man
(the soul; the real personality)

That he would grant you, according to the riches of his glory, to be strengthened with might by his Spirit in **the inner man**; (Ephesians 3:16)

jot or tittle
(the smallest amount; nothing)

For verily I say unto you, Till heaven and earth pass, **one jot or one tittle** shall in no wise pass from the law, till all be fulfilled. (Matthew 5:18)

joy cometh in the morning
(blessing comes after suffering)

For his anger *endureth but* a moment; in hi favour *is* life: weeping may endure for a night, but **joy *cometh* in the morning**. (Psalm 30:5)

kick against the pricks
(to rebel and not face the truth)

And he said, Who art thou, Lord? And the Lord said, I am Jesus whom thou persecutest: *it is* hard for thee **to kick against the pricks**. (Acts 9:5)

king of terrors
(death personified)

His confidence shall be rooted out of his tabernacle, and it shall bring him to **the king of terrors**. (Job 18:14)

laborer is worthy of his hire
(a worker deserves his wages)

And in the same house remain, eating and drinking such things as they give: for **the labourer is worthy of his hire**. Go not from house to house. (Luke 10:7)

land of Nod
(a state of deep sleep)

¶ And Cain went out from the presence of the LORD, and dwelt in **the land of Nod**, on the east of Eden. (Genesis 4:16)

laugh to scorn
(ridicule in contempt)

All they that see me **laugh me to scorn**: they shoot out the lip, they shake the head, *saying*, (Psalm 22:7)

law of the Medes and Persians
(that which can't be changed)

Now, O king, establish the decree, and sign the writing, that it be not changed, according to **the law of**

the Medes and Persians, which altereth not. (Daniel 6:8)

length and breadth of the land, through
   (the whole land)

   Arise, walk through **the land in the length of it and in the breadth** of it; for I will give it unto thee. (Genesis 13:17)

let the dead bury their dead
   (let others do their own business)

   But Jesus said unto him, Follow me; and **let the dead bury their dead**. (Matthew 8:22)

lighten one's darkness
   (to cheer up and encourage)

   For thou *art* my lamp, O LORD: and the LORD will **lighten my darkness**. (2 Samuel 22:29)

like a lamb to the slaughter
   (go quietly in the face of punishment)

   He was oppressed, and he was afflicted, yet he opened not his mouth: he is brought **as a lamb to the slaughter**, and as a sheep before her shearers is dumb, so he openeth not his mouth. (Isaiah 53:7)

lion shall lie down with the lamb
   (a future peace hoped for)

   The wolf and the lamb shall feed together, and the lion shall eat straw like the bullock: and dust *shall be* the serpent's meat. They shall not hurt nor destroy in all my holy mountain, saith the LORD. (Isaiah 65:25)

loaves and fishes

(being religious for any monetary gain)

Then he took the five **loaves and the two fishes**, and looking up to heaven, he blessed them, and brake, and gave to the disciples to set before the multitude. (Luke 9:16)

look on the wine when it's red
(get drunk)

Look not thou upon the wine when it is red, when it giveth his colour in the cup, *when* it moveth itself aright (Proverbs 23:31)

make bricks out of straw
(to attempt a project without what one needs)

Ye shall **no more** give the people **straw to make brick**, as heretofore: let them go and gather straw for themselves. (Exodus 5:7)

make glad the heart of man
(help the heart)

And wine *that* **maketh glad the heart of man**, *and* oil to make *his* face to shine, and bread *which* strengtheneth man's heart. (Psalm 104:15)

many are called, but few are chosen (chosen few)
(only the strong survive)

For **many are called, but few *are* chosen**. (Matthew 22:14)

mark of the beast
(an omen of evil)

And the beast was taken, and with him the false prophet that wrought miracles before him, with which he deceived them that had received **the mark of the beast**, and them that worshipped his image. These both were cast alive into a lake of fire burning with brimstone. (Revelation 19:20)

meek shall inherit the earth
(God's people will own the world)

But **the meek shall inherit the earth**; and shall delight themselves in the abundance of peace. (Psalm 37:11)

mote in the eye
(accusing others of faults that you have)

And why beholdest thou the **mote that is in thy brother's eye**, but considerest not the beam that is in thine own eye? (Matthew 7:3)

move and have your being
(living or existing somewhere)

For in him we **live, and move, and have our being**; as certain also of your own poets have said, For we are also his offspring. (Acts 17:28)

nail someone to the cross
(prove, accuse, or punish another)

Blotting out the handwriting of ordinances that was against us, which was contrary to us, and took it out of the way, **nailing to his cross**; (Colossians 2:14)

no respecter of persons
(to give no special treatment to anyone)

¶ Then Peter opened *his* mouth, and said, Of a truth I perceive that God is **no respecter of persons**: (Acts 10:34)

of the earth, earthy
(physical, material)

The first man *is* **of the earth, earthy**: the second man *is* the Lord from heaven. (1 Corinthians 15:47)

old Adam
(corrupt human nature)

Knowing this, that our **old man** is crucified with *him*, that the body of sin might be destroyed, that henceforth we should not serve sin. (Romans 6:6)

old wine into new bottles
(putting a new package on old material)

And no man putteth **new wine into old bottles**: else the new wine doth burst the bottles, and the wine is spilled, and the bottles will be marred: but new wine must be put into new bottles. (Mark 2:22)

one flesh
(united in marriage)

What? know ye not that he which is joined to an harlot is one body? for two, saith he, shall be **one flesh**. (1 Corinthians 6:16)

peace that passeth all understanding
(peace of mind)

And the **peace of God, which passeth all understanding**, shall keep your hearts and minds through Christ Jesus. (Phillipians 4:7)

Physician, heal thyself
(take care of your own problems)

And he said unto them, Ye will surely say unto me this proverb, **Physician, heal thyself**: whatsoever we have heard done in Capernaum, do also here in thy country. (Luke 4:23)

possess your soul in patience
(to be long-suffering)

In your patience possess ye your souls. (Luke 21:19)

powers of darkness
(evil, Satanic authority)

Who hath delivered us from **the power of darkness**, and hath translated *us* into the kingdom of his dear Son: (Colossians 1:13)

pride goeth before a fall
(pride causes a downfall)

Pride *goeth* before destruction, and an haughty spirit before **a fall**. (Proverbs 16:18)

principalities and powers
(political authorities or high positions)

PUT them in mind to be subject to **principalities and powers**, to obey magistrates, to be ready to every good work. (Titus 3:1)

ravening wolves
(greedy and vicious people)

¶ Beware of false prophets, which come to you in sheep's clothing, but inwardly they are **ravening wolves**. (Matthew 7:15)

reap the whirlwind

(to get into deeper trouble than you expect)

For they have sown the wind, and they shall **reap the whirlwind**: it hath no stalk: the bud shall yield no meal: if so be it yield, the strangers shall swallow it up. (Hosea 8:7)

reed shaken by the wind
(to have an opinion shaped by the times)

¶ And as they departed, Jesus began to say unto the multitudes concerning John, What went ye out into the wilderness to see? **A reed shaken with the wind**? (Matthew 11:7)

riotous living
(a lifestyle of sin)

And not many days after the younger son gathered all together, and took his journey into a far country, and there wasted his substance with **riotous living**. (Luke 15:13)

sackcloth and ashes, put on
(to be repentant and humble)

And in every province, whithersoever the king's commandment and his decree came, *there was* great mourning among the Jews, and fasting, and weeping, and wailing; and many lay in **sackcloth and ashes**. (Esther 4:3)

sell your birthright
(give up all your claim to something)

And Jacob said, Swear to me this day; and he sware unto him: and he **sold his birthright** unto Jacob. (Genesis 25:33)

set your face against
(to turn your mind against something or someone)

And I will **set my face against** that man, and will cut him off from among his people; because he hath given of his seed unto Molech, to defile my sanctuary, and to profane my holy name. (Leviticus 20:3)

shining light
(a prominent individual)

He was a burning and **a shining light**: and ye were willing for a season to rejoice in his light. (John 5:35)

sin will find you out
(your bad deeds will be found out)

But if ye will not do so, behold, ye have sinned against the LORD: and be sure your **sin will find you out**. (Numbers 32:23)

sitting at the receipt of custom
(a money handler or cashier)

¶ And as Jesus passed forth from thence, he saw a man, named Matthew, **sitting at the receipt of custom**: and he saith unto him, Follow me. And he arose, and followed him. (Matthew 9:9)

slow to anger
(a good temperament; even keeled)

And refused to obey, neither were mindful of thy wonders that thou didst among them; but hardened their necks, and in their rebellion appointed a captain to return to their bondage: but thou *art* a God ready to pardon, gracious and merciful, **slow to anger**, and of great kindness, and forsookest them not. (Nehemiah 9:17)

small beginnings
(something not significant at first)

Though thy **beginning was small**, yet thy latter end should greatly increase. (Job 8:7)

smite them hip and thigh
(to savagely attack your enemies with anything)

And he **smote them hip and thigh** with a great slaughter: and he went down and dwelt in the top of the rock Etam. (Judges 15:8)

son of Belial
(a vile, wicked person)

¶ Now the sons of Eli *were* **sons of Belial**; they knew not the LORD.

sounding brass
(one who is all talk; a vain person)

THOUGH I speak with the tongues of men and of angels, and have not charity, I am become *as* **sounding brass**, or a tinkling cymbal. (1 Corinthians 13:1)

spirit is willing, but the flesh is weak
(desire without willpower)

Watch and pray, that ye enter not into temptation: **the spirit indeed *is* willing, but the flesh *is* weak**. (Matthew 26:41)

spoil the Egyptians
(ravage one's enemies)

But every woman shall borrow of her neighbour, and of her that sojourneth in her house, jewels of silver, and jewels of gold, and raiment: and ye shall put *them* upon your sons, and upon your daughters; and ye shall **spoil the Egyptians**. (Exodus 3:22)

still small voice
(listening to your conscience)

And after the earthquake a fire; *but* the LORD *was* not in the fire: and after the fire **a still small voice**. (1 Kings 19:12)

strain at a gnat and swallow a camel
(to trivialize important matters)

Ye blind guides, which **strain at a gnat, and swallow a camel**. (Matthew 23:24)

tell it not in Gath
(don't make something public knowledge)

Tell *it* **not in Gath**, publish *it* not in the streets of Askelon; lest the daughters of the Philistines rejoice, lest the daughters of the uncircumcised triumph. (2 Samuel 1:20)

thief in the night
(secretly; discreetly)

For yourselves know perfectly that the day of the Lord so cometh as **a thief in the night**. (1 Thessalonians 5:2)

tower of strength
(someone you can count on)

The name of the LORD *is* **a strong tower**: the righteous runneth into it, and is safe. (Proverbs 18:10)

valley of the shadow death
(to be near death)

Yea, though I walk through **the valley of the shadow of death**, I will fear no evil: for thou *art* with me; thy rod and thy staff they comfort me. (Psalm 23:4)

very present help in time of trouble
(useful in time of need)

God *is* our refuge and strength, **a very present help in trouble**. (Psalm 46:1)

wars and rumors of wars
(actual war or news of it)

And ye shall hear of **wars and rumours of wars**: see that ye be not troubled: for all *these things* must come to pass, but the end is not yet. (Matthew 24:6)

way of the transgressor is hard
(the hard life of sin)

Good understanding giveth favour: but **the way of transgressors *is* hard**. (Proverbs 13:15)

weariness of the flesh
(something that tires you greatly)

And further, by these, my son, be admonished: of making many books *there is* no end; an much study *is* a **weariness of the flesh**. (Ecclesiastes 12:12)

well nigh
(almost)

But as for me, my feet were almost gone; my steps had **well nigh** slipped. (Psalms 73:2)

whited sepulchre
(a hypocrite, especially religious)

Woe unto you, scribes and Pharisees, hypocrites! for ye are like unto **whited sepulchres**, which indeed appear beautiful outward, but are within full of dead *men's* bones, and of all uncleanness. (Matthew 23:27)

wings of the wind
(go at top speed rather quietly)

And he rode upon a cherub, and did fly: yea, he did fly upon the **wings of the wind**. (Psalm 18:10)

woman's glory
(long hair of a woman)

But if **a woman** have long hair, it is a **glory** to her: for *her* hair is given her for a covering. (1 Corinthians 11:15)

word in season
(saying the right thing at the right time)

A man hath joy by the answer of his mouth: and **a word** *spoken* **in** due **season**, how good *is it*! (Proverbs 15:23)

Appendix B
Popular Expressions
Alluded to in the Bible

all decked out
> (dressed up fancily)

> And I will visit upon her the days of Baalim, wherein she burned incense to them, and **she decked herself** with her earrings and her jewels, and she went after her lovers, and forgat me, saith the LORD. (Hosea 2:13)

all hope is lost
> (an irreversible situation)

> Now when she saw that she had waited, *and* her **hope was lost**, then she took another of her whelps, *and* made him a young lion. (Ezekiel 19:5)

all over but the shouting
> (just about finished)

> For the Lord himself shall **descend from heaven with a shout**, with the voice of the archangel and with the trump of God: and the dead in Christ shall rise first: (1 Thessalonians 4:16)

as a tree falls, so shall it lay
> (an expected happening)

> If the clouds be full of rain, they empty *themselves* upon the earth: and if the tree fall toward the south, or toward the north, in the place **where the tree falleth, there it shall be**. (Ecclesiastes 11:3)

as long as there is life, there is hope
(always believe)

¶ For to him that is joined to all **the living there is hope**: for a living dog is better than a dead lion. (Ecclesiastes 9:4)

at peace with the world
(contented with life)

When a man's ways please the LORD, he maketh even his enemies to be **at peace with him**. (Proverbs 16:7)

beat the hell out of someone
(hurt someone badly)

Thou shalt **beat him** with the rod, and shalt deliver his soul **from hell**. (Proverbs 23:14)

between a rock and a hard place
(two alternatives equally tough)

¶ And between the passages, by which Jonathan sought to go over unto the Philistines' garrison, *there was* **a sharp rock on the one side, and a sharp rock on the other side**: and the name of the one was Bozez, and the name of the other Seneh. (1 Samuel 14:4)

blind faith
(believing without seeing)

NOW **faith is** the substance of things hoped for, **the evidence of things not seen**. (Hebrews 11:1)

blow your own horn
(boast of your accomplishments or self)

Therefore when thou doest *thine* alms, do not **sound a trumpet before thee**, as the hypocrites do in the synagogues and in the streets, that they may have glory of men. Verily I say unto you, They have their reward. (Matthew 6:2)

born to be wild
(natural inclinations for rebellion)

Yet man is **born** un**to trouble**, as the sparks fly upward. (Job 5:7)

bosom buddy
(close, dear friend)

Now there was leaning on Jesus' **bosom one of his disciples**, whom Jesus loved. (John 13:23)

bring down to earth
(make someone face reality)

¶ The pride of thine heart hath deceived thee, thou that dwelleth in the clefts of the rock, whose habitation is high; that saith in his heart, Who shall **bring me down to the ground**? (Obadiah 3)

burn the midnight oil
(work late into the night)

And at **midnight** there was a cry made, Behold, the bridegroom cometh; go ye out to meet him. Then all the virgins arose, and trimmed their lamps. And the foolish said unto the wise, Give us of your **oil**; for our lamps are gone out. (Matthew 25:6-8)

can't call your soul your own
(to have you or your things controlled by others)

What? know ye not that your body is the temple of the Holy Ghost *which is* in you, which ye have of God, and **ye are not your own**? (1 Corinthians 6:19)

can't keep a good man down
(determined to not give up)

The steps of **a good man** are ordered by the Lord, and he delighteth in his ways. Though he fall, he **shall not be utterly cast down**: for the LORD upholdeth *him with* his hand. (Psalm 37:24-5)

can't see for the tears
(crying extensively)

Mine eyes do fail with tears, my bowels are troubled, my liver is poured upon the earth, for the destruction of the daughter of my people; because the children and the sucklings swoon in the streets of the city. (Lamentations 2:11)

can't tell whether it's comin' or goin'
(lost or confused)

The wind bloweth where it listeth, and thou heareth the sound thereof, but **canst not tell whence it cometh, and whither it goeth**: so is every one that is born of the Spirit. (John 3:8)

captain of your soul
(you determine your own fate)

For it became him, for whom *are* all things, and by whom *are* all things, in bringing many sons unto glory, to make **the captain of their salvation** perfect through sufferings. (Hebrews 2:10)

charity begins at home
(take care of your family first)

But if any widow have children or nephews, let them learn first to shew piety **at home, and to requite their parents**: for that is good and acceptable before God. (1 Timothy 5:4)

cover with a fig leaf
(to be chaste; to conceal the flesh)

And the eyes of them both were opened, and they knew that they *were* naked; and **they sewed fig leaves** together, **and made themselves aprons**. (Genesis 3:7)

cross my heart and hope to die
(kill me if I'm wrong)

And when all the people came to cause David to eat meat while it was yet day, David sware, saying, **So do God to me, and more also**, if I taste bread, or ought else, till the sun be down. (2 Samuel 3:35)

dead end
(no improvement possible)

What fruit had ye then in those things whereof ye are now ashamed? for **the end of those things *is* death**. (Romans 6:21)

dead men tell no tales
(the dead can't reveal matters)

For the living know that they shall die: but **the dead know not any thing**, neither have they any more a reward; for the memory of them is forgotten. (Ecclesiastes 9:5)

devil made me do it
(blaming others for your problems)

And the LORD God said unto the woman, What *is* this *that* thou hast done? And the woman said, **The serpent beguiled me, and I did eat**. (Genesis 3:13)

dig your own grave
(cause your own downfall or death)

He that diggeth a pit shall fall into it; and whoso breaketh an hedge, a serpent shall bite him. (Ecclesiastes 10:8)

do as I say, not as I do
(listen, but don't act like me)

All therefore whatsoever they bid you observe, *that* observe and do; but do not ye after their works: for **they say, and do not**. (Matthew 23:3)

do the little things
(giving attention to small matters)

He that is **faithful in that which is least** is faithful also in much: and he that is unjust in the least is unjust also in much. (Luke 16:10)

do unto others
(treat way you want to be treated)

And as ye would that men should do to you, **do ye also to them likewise**. (Luke 6:31)

do your own thing
(follow your own dictates)

In those days *there was* no king in Israel, *but* **every man did *that which was* right in his own eyes**. (Judges 17:6)

doubting Thomas

(someone who is always skeptical)

But Thomas, one of the twelve, called Didymus, was not with them when Jesus came. The other disciples therefore said unto him, We have seen the Lord. But he **said unto them**, **Except I shall see in his hands the print of the nails**, and put my finger into the print of the nails, and thrust my hand into his side**, I will not believe**. (John 20:24-5)

down in the mouth
(a sad countenance)

And the LORD said unto Cain, Why art thou wroth? And why is thy **countenance fallen**?   (Genesis 4:6)

drive you to your knees
(make someone suffer)

Terrors shall make him afraid on every side, and shall **drive him to his feet**. (Job 18:11)

every man for himself
(look out for your own self)

(*For* the men of war had taken spoil, **every man for himself**.) (Numbers 31:53)

eyes are the windows of the soul
(the eyes reveal things)

The light of the body is the eye: if therefore thine eye be single, thy whole body shall be full of light. (Matthew 6:22)

eyes of faith
(spiritual faith)

(For **we walk by faith, not by sight**:) (2 Corinthians 5:7)

eyes on the prize
(focused on a goal)

I press toward the mark for the prize of the high calling of God in Christ Jesus. (Phillipians 3:14)

faith that moves mountains
(strong faith)

And Jesus said unto them, Because of your unbelief: for verily I say unto you, **If ye have faith** as a grain of mustard seed, **ye shall say unto this mountain, Remove hence to yonder place**; and it shall remove; and nothing shall be impossible unto you. (Matthew 17:20)

fate worse than death
(damnation of hell)

And **fear not them which kill the body**, but are not able to kill the soul: but rather **fear him which is able to destroy both soul and body in hell**. (Matthew 10:28)

father knows best
(the parent knows children's needs)

Be not ye therefore like unto them: for **your Father knoweth** what things ye have need of, before ye ask him. (Matthew 6:8)

forbidden fruit
(that which is forbidden yet tempting)

But of **the fruit of the tree** which is in the midst of the garden, God hath said, **Ye shall not eat of it**, neither shall ye touch it, lest ye die. (Genesis 3:3)

full of yourself
(conceited)

The backslider in heart **shall be filled with his own ways**: and a good man *shall be satisfied* from himself. (Proverbs 14:14)

go the extra mile
(give extra effort)

And whosoever shall compel thee to **go a mile, go with him twain**. (Matthew 5:41)

go through the motions
(mechanical, unemotional activity)

For **when we were in the flesh, the motions of sins**, which were by the law, did work in our members to bring forth fruit unto death. (Romans 7:5)

go to your reward
Therefore when thou doest *thine* alms, do not sound a trumpet before thee, as the hypocrites do in the synagogues and in the streets, that they may have glory of men. Verily I say unto you, They **have their reward**. (Matthew 6:2)

good Samaritan
(someone who helps others in need)

But **a certain Samaritan**, as he journeyed, came where he was: and when he saw him, he **had compassion on him**. (Luke 10:33)

have nothing on someone

(to have no accusations on another)

Hereafter I will not talk much with you: for the prince of this world cometh, and **hath nothing in me**. (John 14:30)

haven't got a prayer
(hopeless)

Thou hast covered thyself with a cloud, that **our prayer should not pass through**. (Lamentations 3:44)

he thinks he's something
(arrogant individual)

For **if a man think himself to be something**, when he is nothing, he deceiveth himself. (Galatians 6:3)

he who laughs last laughs best
(final revenge)

He that sitteth in the heavens shall laugh: the Lord shall have them in derision. (Psalm 2:4)

hear no evil, see no evil, speak no evil
(not involved)

For he that will love life, and see good days, **let him refrain his tongue from evil, and his lips that they speak no guile.** (1 Peter 3:10)

hearing footsteps
(listening for those behind you)

But Elisha sat in his house, and the elders sat with him; and *the king* sent a man from before him: but ere the messenger came to him, he said to the elders, See ye how this son of a murderer hath sent to take away mine head? look, when the messenger cometh, shut the door, and hold him fast at the door: *is* not **the sound of his master's feet behind him?** (2 Kings 6:32)

heaven's gate
(entrance to heaven)

And he was afraid, and said, How dreadful *is* this place! this *is* none other but the house of God, and this *is* **the gate of heaven**. (Genesis 28:17)

here today, gone tomorrow
(temporal, fleeting)

Wherefore, if God so clothe the grass of the field, **which to day is, and to morrow is cast into the oven**, *shall he* not much more *clothe* you, O ye of little faith? (Matthew 6:30)

he's asking for it
(looking for trouble)

A fool's lips enter into contention, and **his mouth calleth for strokes**. (Proverbs 18:6)

he's got the whole world in his hands
(have it made)

In whose hand *is* the soul of every living thing, and the breath of all mankind. (Job 12:10)

history repeats itself
(cyclical repetition of events)

The thing that hath been, it *is that* which shall be; and that which is done *is* that which shall be done: and *there is* no new *thing* under the sun. (Ecclesiastes 1:9)

keep body and soul together
  (keep yourself fit)

> And the very God of peace sanctify you wholly; and I *pray God* your whole spirit and **soul and body be preserved blameless** unto the coming of our Lord Jesus Christ. (1 Thessalonians 5:23)

king of the mountain
  (ruler or leader)

> And many people shall go up and say, Come ye, and let us go up to **the mountain of the LORD**, to the house of the God of Jacob; and he will teach us of his ways, and we will walk in his paths: for out of Zion shall go forth the law, and the word of the LORD from Jerusalem. (Psalm 48:2)

kiss of death
  (the coup de grace)

> Now **he that betrayed him gave them a sign, saying, Whomsoever I shall kiss**, that same is he: hold him fast. (Matthew 26:48)

know of what you speak
  (learned)

> Verily, verily, I say unto thee, **We speak that we do know**, and testify that we have seen; and ye receive not our witness. (John 3:11)

laughter is the best medicine
  (humor is good for you)

> **A merry heart doeth good** *like* **a medicine**: but a broken spirit drieth the bones. (Proverbs 17:22)

life's a bitch and then you die
(life is hard with no reward)

This *is* an evil among all *things* that are done under the sun, that *there is* one event unto all: yea, also the heart of the sons of men is full of evil, and and **madness *is* in their heart while they live, and after that *they go* to the dead**. (Ecclesiastes 9:3)

like produces like
(expected results)

And God said, let the earth bring forth grass, the herb yielding seed, *and* **the fruit tree yielding fruit after his kind**, whose seed *is* in itself, upon the earth: and it was so. (Genesis 1:11)

long arm of the law
(authority figure)

Yet they *are* thy people and thine inheritance, which thou broughtest out by thy mighty power and **by thy stretched out arm**. (Deuteronomy 9:29)

look out for yourself
(selfish interests only)

Yea, *they are* greedy dogs *which* can never have enough, and they *are* shepherds that cannot understand: **they all look to their own way**, every one for his gain, from his quarter. (Isaiah 56:11)

man of few words
(a reserved individual)

Be not rash with thy mouth, and let not thine heart be hasty to utter *any* thing before God: for God *is* in heaven, and thou upon earth: therefore **let thy words be few**. (Ecclesiastes 5:2)

marked man
(a person targeted for something)

And the LORD said unto him, Therefore whosoever slayeth Cain, vengeance shall be taken on him sevenfold, **And the LORD set a mark upon Cain**, lest any finding him should kill him. (Genesis 4:15)

marriage made in heaven
(a perfect marriage)

And he saith unto me, Write, Blessed *are* they which are called unto **the marriage supper of the Lamb**. And he saith unto me, These are the true sayings of God. (Revelation 19:9)

mountain top experience
(spiritual encounter)

AND after six days Jesus taketh Peter, James, and John his brother, and **bringeth them up into an high mountain apart. And was transfigured before them**: and his face did shine as the sun, and his raiment was white as the light. (Matthew 17:1-2)

move heaven and earth
(produce almost impossible results)

And **the heaven departed** as a scroll when it is rolled together; **and every mountain and island were moved** out of their places. (Revelation 6:14)

music soothes the savage beast
(goodness tempers evil)

Let our lord now command thy servants, *which are* before thee, to seek out a man, *who is* a cunning player on an harp: and it shall come to pass, **when** the evil spirit from God is upon thee, that he shall play with his hand, and thou shalt be well. (1 Samuel 16:16)

no big deal
(not overly important)

Therefore *it is* no great thing if his ministers also be transformed as the ministers of righteousness; whose end shall be according to their works. (2 Corinthians 11:15)

no pain, no gain
(no sacrifice, no achieving)

If we suffer, we shall also reign with *him*: if we deny *him*, he also will deny us: (2 Timothy 2:12)

none so blind as those who won't see
(purposeful ignorance)

And Jesus said, For judgment I am come into this world, that they which see not might see; and that they which see might be made blind. (John 9:39)

play with fire
(involve yourself with danger)

Can a man take fire in his bosom, and his clothes not be burned? (Proverbs 6:27)

pocket with holes in it
(spending and not saving)
Ye have sown much, and bring in little; ye eat, but ye have not enough; ye drink, but ye are not filled with drink; ye clothe you, but there in none warm; and he that earneth wages earneth wages *to put it* into a bag with holes. (Haggai 1:6)

put out to pasture
(put out of commission)

And they shall drive thee from men, and thy dwelling *shall be* **with the beasts of the field: they shall make thee to eat grass** as oxen, and seven times shall pass over thee, until thou know that the most High ruleth in the kingdom of men, and giveth it to whomsoever he will. (Daniel 4:32)

put someone's lights out
(to stop another completely)

The light of the righteous rejoiceth: but **the lamp of the wicked shall be put out**. (Proverbs 13:9)

rest in peace
(die or be left alone)

Therefore did my heart rejoice, and my tongue was glad; moreover also **my flesh shall rest in hope**. (Acts 2:26)

return to the fold
(come back to a group)

And I will gather the remnant of my flock out of all countries whither I have driven them, and **will bring them again to their folds**; and they shall be fruitful and increase. (Jeremiah 23:3)

sadder but wiser
(knowledge through sadness)
For in much wisdom *is* much grief: and **he that increaseth knowledge increaseth sorrow**. (Ecclesiastes 1:18)

scrape the bottom of the barrel
(barely make ends meet)

And she said, *As* the LORD thy God liveth, I have not a cake, **but an handful of meal in a barrel**, and a little oil in a cruse: and, behold, I *am* gathering two sticks, that I may go in and dress it for me and my son, that we may eat it, and die. (1 Kings 17:2)

second coming
(Jesus' return; resurrection)

And if I go and prepare a place for you, **I will come again**, and receive you unto myself; that where I am, *there* ye may be also. (John 14:3)

seeing is believing
(proof through actually seeing)

The other disciples therefore said unto him, We have seen the Lord. But he said unto them, **Except I shall see** in his hands the print of the nails, and put my finger into the print of the nails, and thrust my hand into his side, **I will not believe**.   (John 20:25)

sick at the sight of someone
(to despise another)

Behold, the hope of him is in vain: **shall not *one* be cast down even at the sight of him**? (Job 41:9)

stink in your nostrils
(abhor something)

I have sent among you the pestilence after the manner of Egypt: your young men have I slain with the sword, and have taken away your horses; and I **have made the stink of your camps to come up unto your nostrils**: yet have ye not returned unto me, saith the LORD. (Amos 4:10)

take the bitter with the sweet
(take the good with the bad)

And I went unto the angel, and said unto him, Give me the little book. And he said unto me, Take *it*, and eat it up; and **it shall make thy belly bitter, but it shall be in thy mouth sweet as honey**. (Revelation 10:9)

there is a time and place for everything
(there is a set time for all endeavors)

TO **every *thing there is* a season**, and a time to every purpose under the heaven: (Ecclesiastes 3:1)

tomorrow will take care of itself
(the future will come regardless)

Take therefore no thought for the morrow: for **the morrow shall take thought for the things of itself**. Sufficient unto the day *is* the evil thereof. (Matthew 6:34)

too much of a good thing is bad
(excess is harmful)

It is **not good to eat much honey**: so *for men* to search their own glory *is not* glory. (Proverbs 25:27)

turn a deaf ear
(not listen)

He that turneth away his ear from hearing law, even his prayer *shall be* abomination. (Proverbs 28:9)

water under the bridge
(forgotten grief)

Because **thou shalt forget** *thy* misery, **and remember it as waters** *that* **pass away**. (Job 11:16)

what's it to you?
(asking the relevance of a matter)

Saying, I have sinned in that I have betrayed the innocent blood. And they said, **What** *is that* **to us**? See thou *to that*. (Matthew 27:4)

when the spirit moves you
(when you feel like it)

And **the spirit of the Lord began to move him** at times in the camp of Dan between Zorah and Eshtaol. (Judges 13:25)

which ever way the wind blows
(swayed easily)

The wind bloweth where it listeth, and thou hearest the sound thereof, but canst not tell whence it cometh, and whither it goeth: so is every one that is born of the Spirit. (John 3:8)

wish you'd never been born
(despise your life)

The Son of man indeed goeth, as it is written of him: but woe to that man by whom the Son of man is betrayed! **good were it for that man if he had never been born**. (Mark 14:21)

woman's place is in the home
(women should work in the home)

I will therefore, that **the younger women marry, bear children, guide the house**, give none occasion to the adversary to speak reproachfully. (1 Timothy 5:14)

wouldn't trust him to watch my dog
(not trust someone at all)

BUT now *they that are* younger than I have me in derision, whose fathers **I would have disdained to have set with the dogs of my flock**. (Job 30:1)

you can't take it with you
(no possessions in heaven)

For we brought nothing into *this* world, *and **it is** certain we can carry nothing out*. (1 Timothy 6:7)

Appendix C
Popular Biblical Expressions in Movie and TV Titles

Amy Prentiss-Baptism of Fire (1974) Jessica Walter,
    William Shatner
And Nothing But the Truth (1982) Glenda Jackson,
    Jon Finch
Blind Faith (1988) Shelley Hack, Jack Langedyk
Body and Soul (1981) Mohammed Ali, Leon Kennedy,
    Peter Lawford
Born Again (1978) Dean Jones, Anne Francis
Brotherly Love (1969) Peter O'Toole, Sussanah York
Brother's Keeper (1992) Joe Berlinger, Bruce Sinofsky
Burnt Offerings (1976) Bette Davis, Burgess Meredith
Call It a Day (1937) Olivia de Havilland, Ian Hunter
Cry in the Wilderness (1974) George Kennedy, Paul
    Sorenson
Dead and Buried (1981) James Farentino, Jack Albertson
Dead End (1937) Joel McCrea, Humphrey Bogart
Dead Men Tell No Tales (1971) Christopher George,
    Judy Carne
Dead to the World (1961) Reedy Talton, Jana Pearce
Death Sentence (1974) Cloris Leachman, Laurence
    Luckinbill
Dirty Money (1972) Alain Delon, Catherine Deneuve,
    Richard Crenna
Don't Take It to Heart (1945) Richard Greene, Patricia
    Medina
Don't Turn the Other Cheek (1973) Franco Nero,
    Lynn Redgrave
Doubting Thomas (1935) Will Rogers, Billie Burke
End of the World (1977) Christopher Lee, Sire Lyon,
    Lew Ayers
Ends of the Earth (1981) Chuck Norris, Christopher Lee
Every Man for Himself (1980) Jacques Dutronc

Evil Eye, The (1964) John Saxon, Leticia Roman
Evil (Under the Sun) (1982) Peter Ustinov, Roddy
    McDowell
Eye for an Eye, An (1996) Sally Field
Eye of the Needle (1981) Donald Sutherland, Kate
    Nelligan
Face to Face (1976) Liv Ullman, Erland Josephson
Fallen Angel (1981) Richard Massur, Dana Hill
Falling from Grace (1992) John Mellencamp, Mariel
    Hemingway
Fire Down Below (1957) Rita Hayworth, Robert
    Mitchum
First Love (1977) William Kaat, Susan Dey, John Heard
Flesh and Blood (1985) Jennifer Leigh, Tom Burlinson
Forbidden Fruit (1958) Fernandel, Francoise Arnoul
Good Fight, The (1992) Christine Lahti, Terry O'Quinn
Gospel According to Vic, The (1986) TomConti, Helen
    Mirren
Green Pastures, The (1936) Marc Connelly, Rex Ingram
Hand in Hand (1960) Loretta Parey, Philip Needs
He Laughed Last (1956) Frankie Lane, Lucy Marlow
Hear No Evil (1993) Marlee Matlin, Martin Sheen
Heart and Souls (1993) Robert Downey Jr., Charles
    Croden
Heart of the Matter, The (1953) Trevor Howard
Hearts and Minds (1934) Peter Davis, Dir.
Heaven on Earth (1986) R.H. Thompson, Sian Leisa
    Davies
High and the Mighty, The (1954) John Wayne, Claire
    Trevor, Robert Stack
High Noon (1952) Gary Cooper, Grace Kelly
High Time (1960) Bing Crosby, Fabian, Tuesday Weld
Holy Terror (1977) Brooke Shields, Tom Signorelli
House Divided, A (1932) Walter Huston, Kent Douglas
In the Cool of the Day (1963) Peter Finch, Jane Fonda,
    Angela Lansbury
In God We Trust (1980) Marty Feldman, Peter Boyle,
    Richard Pryor
In the Spirit (1990) Marlo Thomas, Peter Falk

Joy in the Morning (1965) Richard Chamberlain, Yvette Mimieux

Judgment Day (1988) Kenneth McLeod, David Anthony Smith

Kiss of Death (1947) Victor Mature, Brian Dunleavy, Richard Widmark

Last Laugh, The (1924) Emil Jannings

Law of the Land (1976) Jim Davis, Barbara Parkins, Don Johnson

Left Hand of God, The (1955) Humphrey Bogart, Gene Tiernes, Lee J. Cobb

Light of Day 1987) Michael J. Fox, Joan Jett, Gena Rowlands

Like Father, Like Son (1987) Dudley Moore, Kirk Cameron

Lost and Found (1979) George Segal, Glenda Jackson, John Candy

Made in Heaven (1987) Timothy Hutton, Kelly McGillis

Man of the House (1995) Chevy Chase, Farrah Fawcett

Man of the World (1931) Carole Lombard, William Powell

Man, Woman, and Child (1983) Martin Sheen, Craig Nelson

Merrily We Go to Hell (1932) Fredric March, Sylvia Sidney, Cary Grant

My Brother's Keeper (1948) Jack Warner, George C. Scott

Next of Kin (1989) Patrick Swayze, Liam Neeson, Adam Baldwin, Helen Hunt

Nothing But the Truth (1941) Bob Hope, Paulette Goddard

Out of Season (1975) Vanessa Redgrave, Cliff Robinson

Out of Sight, Out of Mind (1990) Susan Blakely, Wings Hauser

Out of the Body (1988) Mark Hembrow, Tessa Humphries

Passed Away (1992) Bob Hoskins, Jack Warden

Playing with Fire (1985) Gary Coleman, Cicely Tyson

Promised Land (1988) Keifer Sutherland, Meg Ryan
Quick and the Dead, The (1995) Sharon Stone, Gene
      Hackman
Rest in Pieces (1987) Scott Thompson, Lorin Jean
Rise and Fall of Legs Diamond, The (1960) Ray
      Danton, Karen Steele, Warrren Oates
Rise and Shine (1941) Walter Brennan, Milton Berle
Sacred Ground (1983) Tim McIntire, Jack Elam
Salt of the Earth (1954) Will Greer, Mervin Williams
Samaritan: The Mitch Snyder Story (1972) Barry
      Norman, Anne Karina
Saving Grace (1986) Tom Conti, Fernando Rey
Sign o' the Times (1987) Prince, Sheila E., Sheena
      Easton
Sins of the Fathers (1986) Burt Lancaster, Julie Christie
Smooth Talk (1985) Treat Williams, Laura Dern
Spare the Rod (1961) Max Bygraves, Donald
      Pleaseance
Spirit is Willing, The (1967) Sid Caesar, Vera Miles
Star Trek-Episode 68: Wink of an Eye (1969) William
      Shatner, Leonard Nimoy
They Ran for Their Lives (1969) John Payne, Jim
      Davis
Through a Glass Darkly (1961) Max Von Sydow,
      Harriet Anderson
Turning to Stone (1985) Nicky Guadagni, Shirley
      Douglas
Way of all Flesh, The (1940) Akim Tamiroff, Gladys
      George
You Can't Take It with You (1984) Jason Robards Jr.,
      George Rose

Appendix D
Popular Biblical Expressions
in Song Titles

"**A Cross to Bear**" by Iain Matthews

"**A Little Bird Told Me**" by Evelyn Knight

"**Apple of My Eye**" by Badfinger

"**As God is My Witness**" by Toadstool

"**Baptism by Fire**" by Ann DeJarnett

"**Blink of an Eye**" by Michael McDonald

"**Breach of Promise**" by Pell Mell

"**Bread and Wine**" by Peter Gabriel

"**Break of Dawn**" by Salt-N-PEPA

"**Breaking the Law**" by Judas Priest

"**Brotherly Love**" by Moe Bandy

"**Brother's Keeper**" by 12 Gauge

"**By and By When I Need You**" by New Riders of the Purple Sage

"**By the Book**" by Michael Penn

"**By the Sweat of Your Brow**" by The Heptones

"**Cast the First Stone**" by Angel

"**Crystal Clear**" by The Mighty Lemon Drops

"**Dead and Gone**" by Molly Hatchet

"**Dead End**" by Dead Kennedys

"**Dearly Beloved**" by Fred Astaire

"**Den of Thieves**" by Lizzy Borden

"**Die by the Sword**" by Slayer

"**Drop in the Bucket**" by David Lee Roth

"**Eat My Words**" by Taste

"**End of the World**" by Pet Shop Boys

"**Evil Eye**" by Gino Vanelli

"**Eye for an Eye**" by Corrosion of Conformity

"**Eye to Eye**" by Joan Jett

"**Eyesight to the Blind**" by B.B. King

"**Everybody Plays the Fool**" by The Main Ingredient

"**Faith Can Move Mountains**" by Nat King Cole

"**Fall From Grace**" by Siouxsie and the Banshees
"**Fallen Angel**" by Blue Oyster Cult
"**Falling by the Wayside**" by Ramblers
"**Fear and Loathing at 4th and Butternut**" by John Fahey
"**Fight the Good Fight**" by Triumph
"**Fire and Brimstone**" by Joe Walsh
"**First Love**" by POCO
"**Flesh and Blood**" by Johnny Cash
"**Fly in the Ointment**" by The Faces
"**For God's Sake**" by Cut to the Chase
"**For the Love of Money**" by O'Jays
"**Forty Days and Forty Nights**" by Muddy
         Waters
"**Fuel to the Flame**" by Skeeter Davis
"**Give up the Ghost**" by The Le Roi Brothers
"**Go to Hell**" by Alice Cooper
"**God Save the Queen**" by Sex Pistols
"**Good for Nothing**" by Marlene Dietrich
"**Hard Headed Woman**" by Cat Stevens
"**Heart and Soul**" by Mel Torme
"**Heart of Stone**" by The Rolling Stones
"**Hearts and Minds**" by Ebb Nitzer
"**Heart's Desire**" by The Manhattan Transfer
"**Heaven on Earth**" by ASIA
"**Heavy Heart**" by Heart
"**Here and There**" by Sandbox
"**Here Today and Gone Tomorrow**" by Earth, Wind and Fire
"**High Noon**" by Tex Ritter
"**High Time**" by Styx
"**Hold Your Tongue Dear Sally**" by Andy M. Stewart
"**Hole in My Pocket**" by Rickey Van Shelton
"**Holier Than Thou**" by Metallica
"**Holy Water**" by Soundgarden
"**House Divided**" by Dry Branch Fire Squad
"**Hung the Moon**" by Better than Ezra
"**In God We Trust**" by Those X-Cleavers
"**Iron Hand**" by Dire Straits
"**Ivory Tower**" by Cathy Carr
"**Keep the Faith**" by Michael Jackson

"**Kingdom Come**" by David Bowie
"**Know It All**" by Wes Montgomery
"**Labor of Love**" by Robert Cray
"**Land of Milk and Honey**" by Dizzy Gillespie
"**Land of the Giants**" by Craig Chaquico
"**Land of the Living**" by Don Henley
"**Laughing on Judgment Day**" by Thunder
"**Law of the Land**" by The Temptations
"**Like Father Like Son**" by Rick Springfield
"**Little by Little**" by Alice Cooper
"**Lord, Have Mercy on My Soul**" by Black Oak
        Arkansas
"**Lost and Found**" by The Kinks
"**Love Thy Neighbor**" by Bing Crosby
"**Make a Scene**" by Chris Bell
"**Man of the House**" by Loretta Lynn
"**Man of the World**" by Fleetwood Mac
"**Many a Time**" by Common Man Singers
"**Meet Your Maker**" by Bitter End
"**Mind Your Own Business**" by Hank Williams, Jr.
"**My Cup Runneth Over**" by George Jones
"**My Heart is an Open Book**" by Carl Dobkins, Jr.
"**My Heart's Desire**" by The Earls
"**Name in Vain**" by Motorhead
"**Night is Still Young**" by Billy Joel
"**Nothin' New Under the Sun**" by Inner Circle
"**One Way or Another**" by Blondie
"**Out of Season**" by R.E.O. Speedwagon
"**Out of Sight, Out of Mind**" by Elvis Presley
"**Out of the Body**" by Pestilence
"**Parting of Our Ways**" by Carpenters
"**Passed Away**" by Desultory
"**Passing the Time**" by Cream
"**Patience Like Job**" by Sunnyland Slim Blues Band
"**Patience of a Saint**" by Electronic Band
"**Peace and Quiet Time**" by Mike Fahn
"**Peace of Mind**" by Teresa Brewer
"**Peace on Earth**" by David Bowie and Bing Crosby
"**Pearly Gates**" by Blind Willie MC Tell

"**Putty (in Your Hands)**" by The Shirelles
"**Reap the Whirlwind**" by Don Pullen
"**Reap What You Sow**" by The Pastels
"**Rest for the Weary**" by Marc Cohn
"**Rest in Peace**" by Mott the Hoople
"**Rise and Shine**" by Pink Floyd
"**Root of All Evil**" by Sacred Denial
"**Run For Your Life**" by The Beatles
"**Sackcloth and Ashes**" by The Mr. T.
        Experience
"**Sacred Ground**" by McBride and the Ride
"**Safe and Sound**" by Carly Simon
"**Salt of the Earth**" by Joan Baez
"**Saving Grace**" by Bob Dylan
"**Scum of the Earth**" by The Kinks
"**See the Light**" by Jeff Healey Band
"**Seeing is Believing**" by Mike and the Mechanics
"**Skin O' My Teeth**" by Megadeath
"**Stone's Throw from Hurtin'**" by Elton John
"**Straight and Narrow**" by Paul Overstreet
"**Stranger in a Strange Land**" by U2
"**Streets of Gold**" by The Fabulous Thunderbirds
"**Stumbling Block Blues**" by Champion Jack DuPree
"**Such and Such**" by 7 Seconds
"**Sweatin' Bullets**" by Brand Nubian
"**Take It Easy**" by The Eagles
"**Tell It Like It Is**" by Bad Company
"**Tender Mercies**" by Scott Kempner
"**The Eleventh Hour**" by Mars Lasar
"**The End is Near**" by Leaders of the New School
"**The Extra Mile**" by Tom Russell
"**The Good Lord**" by The Abyssinians
"**The Gospel According to Darkness**" by Jane
        Siberry
"**The Heart of the Matter**" by Kenny Rogers
"**The Heat of the Battle**" by Roy Buchanan
"**The High and the Mighty**" by Leroy Holmes
"**The Powers That Be**" by Roger Waters
"**The Promised Land**" by Chuck Berry

"**The Ten Commandments of Love**" by Little Anthony
     and the Imperials
 "**There is No Greater Love**" by Billie Holiday
"**Thorn in My Side**" by Eurythmics
"**Through a Glass Dimly**" by Jeff Beal
"**To the Ends of the Earth**" by Nat King Cole
"**Tossin' and Turnin'**" by Bobby Lewis
"**Turned to Stone**" by Electric Light Orchestra
"**Two Heads Are Better Than One**" by Power Tool
"**Under My Wings**" by James Taylor
"**Voice in the Wilderness**" by Unshakable Race
"**Wages of Sin**" by Pegboy
"**Walk Hand in Hand**" by Tony Martin
"**Walk on the Water**" by Neil Diamond
"**Woe is Me**" by The Cadillacs
"**Writing on the Wall**" by Ted Nugent
"**Written in Stone**" by Daryl Hall
"**You Can't Take It With You**" by Ray Price
"**Your Days Are Numbered**" by Big Chief
"**You're Breakin' My Heart**" by Vic Damone

JUST SAY THE WORD!
Ordering Information

(Please send order form on next page via fax, e-mail, or regular mail at the following addresses or phone #)

Website address order forms:
www.godstreasurechest.com

Fax order form or phone in order:
Fax: 713-718-6180 Phone: 281-530-9720

E-mail order form to:
godstreasure@ev1.net

Mail order form and payment to:
God's Treasure Chest
P.O. Box 2053
Alief, Texas 77411-2053

Methods of Payment:
U. S. money orders or cashier's checks
Personal check (shipped after it clears)
Cash (please conceal)
VISA or MasterCard

Merchandise Pricing

Just Say the Word!
1-9 copies: $12.95 each
10+copies: $11.95 each

Please make checks payable to:God's Treasure Chest
Mechandise will be shipped when payment is received
Order multiple copies for your church, school, friends, and family and receive the above discounts. All sales final. Sorry, no returns.

God's Treasure Chest
Order Form for *Just Say the Word!*

Your shipping address:

Name:_____

Address:_____

City, State, Zip_____

E-mail:_____Fax and/or phone_____

Quantity of books needed:_____   **Subtotal:_____**
Shipping and Handling
   ($2.50 for one copy)
   ($1.00 for each additional book)   **Ship. & Hand. _____**

Taxes   **Taxes:_____**
(Texas residents add 7.25 %)
(Houston, Texas residents add 8.25%)
(Out of Texas-no taxes)   **Total:_____**
Tax exempt or retailer (provide copy of certificate with this form)

VISA #_____ Exp. Date_____

MasterCard #_____Exp. Date_____

Signature_____

Please make checks payable to: God's Treasure Chest

Mail payment and this order form to:

God's Treasure Chest
P.O. Box 2053
Alief, Texas 77411-2053
Thank you for ordering *Just Say the Word!*